The
Lake English Classics

General Editor
LINDSAY TODD DAMON, A.B.
Professor of
English Literature and Rhetoric in Brown University

The Lake English Classics — continued

SCOTT, FORESMAN AND COMPANY

CHICAGO: 623 Wabash Ave.   NEW YORK: 460 Fourth Ave.

EDMUND BURKE'S *1729?—1797*

SPEECH ON CONCILIATION

WITH AMERICA

1775

N/CBI

EDITED FOR SCHOOL USE

BY

JOSEPH VILLIERS DENNEY
PROFESSOR IN OHIO STATE UNIVERSITY

SCOTT, FORESMAN AND COMPANY
CHICAGO   NEW YORK

CONTENTS

6484

PREFACE

In this edition, the aim of the editor has been to direct the pupil to the logical structure as well as to the literary and rhetorical qualities of the *Speech on Conciliation*. The logical structure, each pupil may discover for himself, by making a brief of the speech as he reads the groups of paragraphs which mark the successive steps in the argument. (See page 132.) The literary and rhetorical qualities are sought through the medium of suggestive questions and topics for individual study. (See page 127.) The Introduction, therefore, does not discuss Burke's style.

The books to which the editor is chiefly indebted are mentioned on page 21, and in the notes. In the preparation of the notes, the editor also acknowledges indebtedness to the long line of editors who have preceded him.

INTRODUCTION

It is no exaggeration to say that they [the *Speech on American Taxation*, the *Speech on Conciliation*, and the *Letter to the Sheriffs of Bristol*] compose the most perfect manual in our literature, or in any literature, for one who approaches the study of public affairs, whether for knowledge or for practice. They are an example without fault of all the qualities which the critic, whether a theorist or an actor, of great political situations should strive by night and by day to possess. If the subject with which they deal were less near than it is to our interests and affections as free citizens, these three performances would still abound in the lessons of an incomparable political method. If their subject were as remote as the quarrel between Corinthians and Corcyra, or the war between Rome and the Allies, instead of a conflict to which the world owes the opportunity of the most important of political experiments, we should still have everything to learn from the author's treatment; the vigorous grasp of masses of compressed detail, the wide illumination from great principles of human experience, the strong and masculine feeling for the two great political ends of Justice and Freedom, the large and generous interpretation of expediency, the morality, the vision, the noble temper.
—*Morley*

INTRODUCTION

EDMUND BURKE

Edmund Burke was born in Dublin in 1729. His father, a lawyer in good practice, was a Protestant; his mother, a Catholic. Edmund was reared a Protestant, but he always respected the faith of his mother, and in after years worked with zeal to secure to his Catholic countrymen their political rights. For two years (1741-1743) he went to school at Ballitore, to Abraham Shackleton, a Quaker, of whose good influence Burke always spoke in the highest terms. Then he went to Trinity College, Dublin, where he remained until he took his degree in 1748. From 1744 to 1749 Oliver Goldsmith was at Trinity, but there is no evidence that he and Burke were acquainted in college, though they were afterwards friends and comrades in London. Burke did not excel in the studies prescribed for him at Trinity, but, following his bent, read widely in natural philosophy, logic, metaphysics, history, and poetry.

His father, intending to make a London lawyer of him. entered him as a student at the Middle Temple; and Burke accordingly took up his residence in London, in 1750. He did not apply himself with diligence to his legal studies, but continued his college habit of reading at large in literature and philosophy, finding time also to attend the theatres and the debating clubs and to travel in England and on the continent. In spite of his neglect of routine legal study Burke somehow gained a wonderful mastery over fundamental legal principles, especially those underlying the science of government. His father however was greatly disappointed at Burke's course in London, stopped the young man's allowance, in 1755, and left him to support himself by writing for the book-sellers. The next year he published two books which won him distinction: *A Vindication of Natural Society*, and *A Philosophical Inquiry into the Origin of Our Ideas on the Sublime and Beautiful*. The same year (1756), he married Jane Nugent, whose calm, even temper, and ability in household management made her unusually helpful to him. Their home life was very happy.

In 1759 began Burke's thirty-year connection with the *Annual Register*, a summary of important events, published by Dodsley. The articles which Burke contributed to this publication marked him at once as a man of keen political insight and broad judgment, and brought him to the notice of the party leaders. From 1761 to 1763, Burke was in Ireland as a secretary to William Gerard Hamilton (who was chief secretary to the Lord Lieutenant), receiving through Hamilton's influence a pension of three hundred pounds. But it soon became evident that what was wanted of Burke was a slavish devotion of all his talents to the fortunes of Hamilton, and Burke indignantly left him, resigned the pension, and returned to the service of Dodsley in London. There he soon became one of the famous Literary Club, which numbered among its members such men as Johnson, Goldsmith, Garrick and Reynolds.

When Lord Rockingham, the leader of a party of Old Whigs or Conservative Whigs, became Prime Minister in 1765, he made Burke his private secretary. In December of the same year, Burke was elected to Parliament from the borough of Wendover, and, very soon after taking his seat in January, 1766, he spoke brilliantly and most effectively in favor of the repeal of the Stamp Act, urging that it was unwise and inexpedient to tax the colonies even if Parliament had a legal right to do so. After the Rockingham ministry was dismissed in 1766, Burke might have held office under Pitt, Rockingham's successor, the leader of the New Whigs or Radical Whigs, but he refused to abandon his political associates for the sake of personal advancement.

In Parliament, Burke did all that he could in opposition to the policy of George the Third, who was trying to make his power absolute. He spoke

against excluding Wilkes from Parliament. Wilkes
had incurred the King's displeasure because of his
radical opinions fearlessly expressed. He had been
repeatedly elected to the House of Commons, and
had been as often kept from his seat by a majority
subservient to the King's wishes. Burke main-
tained the right of the voters to elect whomsoever
they thought fit. As a result of the arbitrary
course pursued by Parliament in the Wilkes affair
there was general discontent among the people, and
some rioting. In 1770, Burke published his
Thoughts on the Cause of the Present Discontents,
in which he averred that all of England's troubles
had arisen from the pursuit of selfish ends by the
King and his secret counsellors, who were breaking
up orderly party government and introducing confusion and disorder. The same year (1770) Lord
North's Tory ministry began its fateful career of
twelve years, at the end of which George the Third
found himself stripped of his American colonies.
During these years, Burke's voice was often heard
in Parliament, warning the King's ministers of
the disasters that would surely follow their arbitrary acts, expounding a philosophy of government
based upon reason and righteousness, trying all
questions by tests of truth. He never relaxed his
efforts, although he knew beforehand that they
were doomed to failure at the hands of a Parliament in control of the "King's friends."

In 1774, Bristol, then the second city in England, elected Burke as its representative in Parliament. Bristol had a large trade with America, and had much to lose if the troubles with the colonies should grow into war. While he was member for Bristol he delivered the *Speech on American Taxation* (April 19, 1774), in which he urged the repeal of the tea tax ; the *Speech on Conciliation with the Colonies* (March 22, 1775) ; and wrote the *Letter to the Sheriffs of Bristol on the Affairs of America* (April 3, 1777), in which he justified his course in Parliament. Burke felt through all these years of war that the cause of liberty in England itself was endangered by the employment of armed force against the colonies. If the King could use an army against Englishmen in the colonies, in a controversy over a question of constitutional right, what was to prevent him from using an army against Englishmen at home whenever in the future they should make a similar claim of constitutional right against him? It was indeed fortunate for English liberty that the colonies were finally victorious. Burke represented Bristol until 1780, when he failed of re-election because, contrary to the narrow and selfish instructions of his constituents, he had voted in favor of a bill to relieve Irish commerce of some grievous restrictions. Burke did not believe that a representative is bound to vote according to the wishes of his constituents if so to vote be against his own judgment of what is right and best. Rejected by

Bristol, he was elected by the borough of Malton.

When, after Yorktown, Lord North's ministry came to an end (1782), the Rockingham party again came into power. Burke now had a right to expect a cabinet office. He was the ablest and most conspicuous member of the party; he had kept it together against the King's efforts to destroy it; he had brought great honor to it by his speeches. Yet he was not admitted to the cabinet, but was appointed to a second-rate position as Paymaster of the Forces. Some of the reasons why it was not considered good politics, in the England of the eighteenth century, to give Burke a cabinet position were his nationality and his obscure origin; his poverty and his debts; his liberal views on the Catholic question; charges (never proved) against his honesty, arising from his close intimacy with relatives of his who were known to have engaged in certain questionable speculations an irritability of temper which increased with age; and the large number of political enemies he had made. For such reasons the first political thinker of the age was set aside by his party associates on the one occasion when they had the opportunity of rewarding him. Burke felt the neglect keenly. Rockingham died in three months. Burke refused office under Shelburne; went into opposition with Fox, Shelburne's rival for the leadership; the Whig party was consequently split in twain, and the Shelburne ministry went to pieces in 1783. Then the Coalition ministry was formed, including such incongruous elements as the Whig, Fox, and the Tory, Lord North, with Burke as Paymaster again. Fox brought in a bill to reform the government of India. Burke advocated the bill, and it passed the House of Commons, but the King, procuring its defeat in the House of Lords, dismissed Fox at the close of 1783. With the advent of the Pitt ministry Burke went out of executive office forever.

Of the three great subjects that engaged Burke's powers during his public career,—America, India, and France,—the second had now become prominent. For many years Burke had studied the history and the workings of English rule in India. He had made himself the best-informed man in England on that subject. He knew that the East India Company had become terribly corrupt and cruel; that it had plundered whole provinces, and had reduced millions of people to wretchedness. He believed that it was now exercising a corrupt influence in Parliament itself. He had no sympathy with the men who had overthrown the native governments in India and had established in their stead an irresponsible system of tyranny. In 1785 he gave expression to some of his indignation and wrath at the condition of affairs in India in his *Speech on the Nabob of Arcot's Debts*. For the policy of Warren Hastings, Governor General

of India, Burke entertained feelings of positive
horror, and in 1786 articles prepared by Burke
impeaching Hastings of high crimes and mis-
demeanors were presented to the House of Commons. The trial of Hastings began in 1788,
Burke making the greatest speech of his life at
the opening (*The Impeachment of Warren
Hastings*). The case was not finally concluded
until 1795, when Hastings was acquitted. The
trial had, however, convinced the nation of the
need of reform in the government of India, and to
Burke's unsuccessful attack on Hastings must be
attributed the improvement that followed in the
government of India.

The French Revolution was the occasion of
Burke's separating from his former Whig associates. Burke, always a conservative, had now
become much more conservative than his party.
The Whigs very generally applauded the Revolution in France, and at one time there was some
danger of a sympathetic outbreak in England.
Burke, however, saw in the Revolution nothing
but destruction. He believed it to be the work of
atheists and theorists who were waging relentless
war upon the institutions which, he thought, preserve order in society,—upon King, Nobles, and
Clergy. It was charged against him that he had
lost his sympathy for the people; that he thought
only of preserving the privileges of the ruling
classes. For the common people of France, who

had suffered a thousand-fold more wrongs than the Americans, Burke had, indeed, no word but obedience. When, in 1790, he published his *Reflections on the Revolution in France*, his old enemies the Tories, King George himself, and all the other arbitrary monarchs in Europe, looked upon Burke as their defender and shield. As the Revolution developed its worst features, Burke's hatred of it grew; he became more violent in temper and less capable of calm discussion. In his subsequent papers on the subject, from the *Letter to a Member of the National Assembly* to the *Letters on a Regicide Peace*, there is a steady decline of those powers of reasoning and persuasion which are seen at their best in the *Speech on Conciliation*.

Burke retired from Parliament three years before his death, having urged for Ireland a policy similar to that which he had urged for America. He was to have been made a peer with the title of Lord Beaconsfield, but the death of his son Richard left him without an heir, and he accepted a pension of £2,500 a year instead of a peerage. His enemies attacked him for taking a pension, and he replied in the *Letter to a Noble Lord*, in which he vindicated his course completely. He died in 1797.

Burke's leading characteristic was a high and noble devotion to principle, regardless of consequences to his own fortunes. Though he loved social order, based on strict justice, he believed in magnanimity in government. He himself was

generous and open-handed in his relations with
others, but careless about incurring debts.   His
desire to live as other men in high position lived
in that day caused him, in 1768, to purchase with
borrowed money an estate costing more than a
hundred thousand dollars,—a piece of extravagance
that led to false insinuations of dishonesty.   Burke
was enthusiastic in working for any cause that he
took up.   His vigor and industry were astonishing.
His reading was prodigious, and his power of
marshalling facts and of filling them with meaning
was extraordinary.   "That fellow calls forth all
my powers," said Dr. Johnson.   Macaulay considered Burke the greatest man since Milton.
Certain it is that few statesmen have ever lived
whose speeches have possessed that quality of
permanence, that value to other generations, which
marks the utterances of Burke.   He who would
attain "large and liberal ideas in politics" should
give Burke thorough study.   Said Fox, "I have
learned more from him than from all the books I
ever read."

A BRIEF BIBLIOGRAPHY

JOHN MORLEY. *Burke* (in the *English Men of Letters Series*). This is the standard biography of Burke.

JOHN MORLEY. *Burke* (in the *Encyclopædia Britannica*).

JOHN MORLEY. *Burke: An Historical Study*. This work deals with Burke's political side alone.

LESLIE STEPHEN. *History of English Thought in the Eighteenth Century*, volume ii. Burke's political theories are carefully set forth in their historical relationships.

DICTIONARY OF NATIONAL BIOGRAPHY. *Burke*. A valuable bibliography is attached to the biography.

AUGUSTINE BIRRELL. *Burke* (in *Obiter Dicta*, second series).

WOODROW WILSON. *The Interpreter of English Liberty* (in *Mere Literature*). A suggestive and entertaining essay. For bibliography of other essays on Burke consult Poole's Index.

The principal events of the controversy with which the *Speech on Conciliation* is concerned are summed up in every good history of the United States (*Fiske, Andrews, Johnston*). They are treated more at length in the following:

W. H. LECKY. *History of England in the Eighteenth Century*.

GEORGE BANCROFT. *A History of the United States*.

HOSMER. *Samuel Adams* (in the *American Statesmen Series*).

J. R. GREEN. *A Short History of the English People*.

In the common principles of all social and civil order, Burke is unquestionably our best and wisest teacher. In handling the particular questions of his time he always involves those principles, and brings them to their practical bearings, where they most "come home to the business and bosoms of men." And his pages are everywhere bright with the highest and purest political morality, while at the same time he is a consummate master in the intellectual charms and graces of authorship —*Hudson.*

SPEECH ON CONCILIATION WITH AMERICA

Perhaps the greatest speech Burke ever made was that on Conciliation with America; the wisest in its temper, the most closely logical in its reasoning, the amplest in appropriate topics, the most generous and conciliatory in the substance of its appeals.—*Morley*.

SPEECH

ON

MOVING HIS RESOLUTIONS

FOR

CONCILIATION WITH THE COLONIES,

MARCH 22, 1775.

---

[1]   I hope, Sir, that, notwithstanding the austerity
of the Chair, your good-nature will incline you to
some degree of indulgence towards human frailty.
You will not think it unnatural, that those who
have an object depending, which strongly engages
their hopes and fears, should be somewhat inclined
to superstition.   As I came into the House full of
anxiety about the event of my motion, I found, to
my infinite surprise, that the grand penal bill, by
which we had passed sentence on the trade and
sustenance of America, is to be returned to us from
the other House.   I do confess, I could not help
looking on this event as a fortunate omen.   I look
upon it as a sort of providential favour; by which
we are put once more in possession of our delibera-
tive capacity, upon a business so very questionable
in its nature, so very uncertain in its issue.   By
the return of this bill, which seemed to have taken

its flight for ever, we are at this very instant nearly as free to choose a plan for our American government as we were on the first day of the session. If, Sir, we incline to the side of conciliation, we are not at all embarrassed (unless we please to make ourselves so) by any incongruous mixture of coercion and restraint.   We are therefore called upon, as it were, by a superior warning voice, again to attend to America; to attend to the whole of it together; and to review the subject with an unusual degree of care and calmness.

[26]   Surely it is an awful subject; or there is none so on this side of the grave. When I first had the honour of a seat in this House, the affairs of that continent pressed themselves upon us, as the most important and most delicate object of parliamentary attention. My little share in this great deliberation oppressed me.   I found myself a partaker in a very high trust; and having no sort of reason to rely on the strength of my natural abilities for the proper execution of that trust, I was obliged to take more than common pains to instruct myself in everything which relates to our colonies.   I was not less under the necessity of forming some fixed ideas concerning the general policy of the British empire.   Something of this sort seemed to be indispensable; in order, amidst so vast a fluctuation of passions and opinions, to concentre my thoughts; to ballast my conduct; to preserve me from being blown about

oy every wind of fashionable doctrine. I really
did not think it safe, or manly, to have fresh principles to seek upon every fresh mail which should
arrive from America.

[3]   At that period I had the fortune to find myself
in perfect concurrence with a large majority in
this House. Bowing under that high authority,
and penetrated with the sharpness and strength of
that early impression, I have continued ever since,
without the least deviation, in my original sentiments. Whether this be owing to an obstinate perseverance in error, or to a religious adherence to
what appears to me truth and reason, it is in your
equity to judge.

4)   Sir, Parliament, having an enlarged view of
objects, made, during this interval, more frequent
changes in their sentiments and their conduct,
than could be justified in a particular person upon
the contracted scale of private information. But
though I do not hazard anything approaching to
censure on the motives of former parliaments to
all those alterations, one fact is undoubted,—that
under them the state of America has been kept in
continual agitation. Everything administered as
remedy to the public complaint, if it did not
produce, was at least followed by, an heightening
of the distemper; until, by a variety of experiments,
that important country has been brought into her
present situation;—a situation which I will not
miscall, which I dare not name; which I scarcely

know how to comprehend in the terms of any description.

[5]   In this posture, Sir, things stood at the beginning of the session. About that time, a worthy member of great parliamentary experience, who, in the year 1766, filled the chair of the American committee with much ability, took me aside; and, lamenting the present aspect of our politics, told me, things were come to such a pass, that our former methods of proceeding in the House would be no longer tolerated. That the public tribunal (never too indulgent to a long and unsuccessful opposition) would now scrutinize our conduct with unusual severity. That the very vicissitudes and shiftings of ministerial measures, instead of convicting their authors of inconstancy and want of system, would be taken as an occasion of charging us with a predetermined discontent, which nothing could satisfy; whilst we accused every measure of vigour as cruel, and every proposal of lenity as weak and irresolute. The public, he said, would not have patience to see us play the game out with our adversaries: we must produce our hand. It would be expected, that those who for many years had been active in such affairs should show, that they had formed some clear and decided idea of the principles of colony government; and were capable of drawing out something like a platform of the ground which might be laid for future and permanent tranquillity.

[6]   I felt the truth of what my honourable friend represented; but I felt my situation, too.   His application might have been made with far greater propriety to many other gentlemen.   No man was indeed ever better disposed, or worse qualified, for such an undertaking, than myself.   Though I gave so far in to his opinion, that I immediately threw my thoughts into a sort of parliamentary form, I was by no means equally ready to produce them.   It generally argues some degree of natural impotence of mind, or some want of knowledge of the world, to hazard plans of government except from a seat of authority.   Propositions are made, not only ineffectually, but somewhat disreputably, when the minds of men are not properly disposed for their reception; and for my part, I am not ambitious of ridicule; not absolutely a candidate for disgrace.

[7]   Besides, Sir, to speak the plain truth, I have in general no very exalted opinion of the virtue of paper government; nor of any politics in which the plan is to be wholly separated from the execution.   But when I saw that anger and violence prevailed every day more and more; and that things were hastening towards an incurable alienation of our colonies; I confess my caution gave way.   I felt this, as one of those few moments in which decorum yields to a higher duty.   Public calamity is a mighty leveller; and there are occasions when any, even the slightest, chance of

doing good, must be laid hold on, even by the
most inconsiderable person.

[8]   To restore order and repose to an empire so great
and so distracted as ours, is, merely in the attempt,
an undertaking that would ennoble the flights of
the highest genius, and obtain pardon for the
efforts of the meanest understanding.   Struggling
a good while with these thoughts, by degrees I
felt myself more firm.   I derived, at length, some
confidence from what in other circumstances
usually produces timidity.   I grew less anxious,
even from the idea of my own insignificance.
For, judging of what you are by what you ought
to be, I persuaded myself that you would not
reject a reasonable proposition because it had nothing but its reason to recommend it.   On the other
hand, being totally destitute of all shadow of influence, natural or adventitious, I was very sure, that,
if my proposition were futile or dangerous; if it
were weakly conceived, or improperly timed, there
was nothing exterior to it, of power to awe, dazzle,
or delude you.   You will see it just as it is: and
you will treat it just as it deserves.

[9]   The proposition is peace.   Not peace through
the medium of war; not peace to be hunted
through the labyrinth of intricate and endless
negotiations; not peace to arise out of universal
discord, fomented from principle, in all parts of
the empire; not peace to depend on the juridical
determination of perplexing questions, or the

precise marking the shadowy boundaries of a complex government. It is simple peace; sought in its natural course, and in its ordinary haunts.—It is peace sought in the spirit of peace; and laid in principles purely pacific. I propose, by removing the ground of the difference, and by restoring the *former unsuspecting confidence of the colonies in the mother country*, to give permanent satisfaction to your people; and (far from a scheme of ruling by discord) to reconcile them to each other in the same act, and by the bond of the very same interest which reconciles them to British government.

[10]   My idea is nothing more. Refined policy ever has been the parent of confusion; and ever will be so, as long as the world endures. Plain good intention, which is as easily discovered at the first view, as fraud is surely detected at last, is, let me say, of no mean force in the government of mankind. Genuine simplicity of heart is an healing and cementing principle. My plan, therefore, being formed upon the most simple grounds imaginable, may disappoint some people, when they hear it. It has nothing to recommend it to the pruriency of curious ears. There is nothing at all new and captivating in it. It has nothing of the splendour of the project, which has been lately laid upon your table by the noble lord in the blue riband. It does not propose to fill your lobby with squabbling colony agents, who will require the interposition of your mace, at every instant, to

keep the peace amongst them. It does not insti-
tute a magnificent auction of finance, where captivated provinces come to general ransom by bidding
against each other, until you knock down the hammer, and determine a proportion of payments beyond
all the powers of algebra to equalize and settle.

[11]   The plan which I shall presume to suggest,
derives, however, one great advantage from the
proposition and registry of that noble lord's project. The idea of conciliation is admissible.
First, the House, in accepting the resolution moved
by the noble lord, has admitted, notwithstanding
the menacing front of our address, notwithstanding our heavy bills of pains and penalties—that we
do not think ourselves precluded from all ideas of
free grace and bounty.

[12]   The House has gone further; it has declared
conciliation admissible, *previous* to any submission
on the part of America. It has even shot a good
deal beyond that mark, and has admitted, that the
complaints of our former mode of exerting the right
of taxation were not wholly unfounded. That
right thus exerted is allowed to have had something
reprehensible in it; something unwise, or something
grievous; since, in the midst of our heat and resent-
ment, we, of ourselves, have proposed a capital altera-
tion; and, in order to get rid of what seemed so very
exceptionable, have instituted a mode that is altogether new; one that is, indeed, wholly alien from
all the ancient methods and forms of parliament.

[13]   The *principle* of this proceeding is large enough for my purpose. The means proposed by the noble lord for carrying his ideas into execution, I think, indeed, are very indifferently suited to the end; and this I shall endeavour to show you before I sit down. But, for the present, I take my ground on the admitted principle. I mean to give peace. Peace implies reconciliation; and, where there has been a material dispute, reconciliation does in a manner always imply concession on the one part or on the other. In this state of things I make no difficulty in affirming that the proposal ought to originate from us. Great and acknowledged force is not impaired, either in effect or in opinion, by an unwillingness to exert itself. The superior power may offer peace with honour and with safety. Such an offer from such a power will be attributed to magnanimity. But the concessions of the weak are the concessions of fear. When such a one is disarmed, he is wholly at the mercy of his superior; and he loses for ever that time and those chances, which, as they happen to all men, are the strength and resources of all inferior power.

[14]   The capital leading questions on which you must this day decide, are these two: First, whether you ought to concede; and secondly, what your concession ought to be. On the first of these questions we have gained (as I have just taken the liberty of observing to you) some ground. But I am sensible that a good deal more is still to be done.

Indeed, Sir, to enable us to determine both on the
one and the other of these great questions with a
firm and precise judgment, I think it may be
necessary to consider distinctly the true nature and
the peculiar circumstances of the object which we
have before us.   Because after all our struggle,
whether we will or not, we must govern America
according to that nature, and to those circumstances; and not according to our own imagina-
tions; nor according to abstract ideas of right; by
no means according to mere general theories of
government, the resort to which appears to me, in
our present situation, no better than arrant trifling.
I shall therefore endeavour, with your leave, to lay
before you some of the most material of these
circumstances in as full and as clear a manner as I
am able to state them.

[15]   The first thing that we have to consider with
regard to the nature of the object is—the number
of people in the colonies.   I have taken for some
years a good deal of pains on that point.   I can by
no calculation justify myself in placing the number
below two millions of inhabitants of our own
European blood and colour; besides at least 500,-
000 others, who form no inconsiderable part of the
strength and opulence of the whole.   This, Sir, is,
I believe, about the true number.   There is no
occasion to exaggerate, where plain truth is of so
much weight and importance.   But whether I put
the present numbers too high or too low, is a mat-

ter of little moment. Such is the strength with which population shoots in that part of the world, that state the numbers as high as we will, whilst the dispute continues, the exaggeration ends. Whilst we are discussing any given magnitude, they are grown to it. Whilst we spend our time in deliberating on the mode of governing two millions, we shall find we have millions more to manage. Your children do not grow faster from infancy to manhood than they spread from families to communities, and from villages to nations.

[16]   I put this consideration of the present and the growing numbers in the front of our deliberation; because, Sir, this consideration will make it evident to a blunter discernment than yours, that no partial, narrow, contracted, pinched, occasional system will be at all suitable to such an object. It will show you, that it is not to be considered as one of those *minima* which are out of the eye and consideration of the law; not a paltry excrescence of the state; not a mean dependent, who may be neglected with little damage, and provoked with little danger. It will prove that some degree of care and caution is required in the handling such an object; it will show that you ought not, in reason, to trifle with so large a mass of the interests and feelings of the human race. You could at no time do so without guilt; and be assured you will not be able to do it long with impunity.

17]   But the population of this country, the great and

growing population, though a very important consideration, will lose much of its weight, if not com-
bined with other circumstances. The commerce of
your colonies is out of all proportion beyond the
numbers of the people. This ground of their
commerce indeed has been trod some days ago,
and with great ability, by a distinguished person,
at your bar. This gentleman, after thirty-five
years—it is so long since he first appeared at the
same place to plead for the commerce of Great
Britain—has come again before you to plead the
same cause, without any other effect of time, than,
that to the fire of imagination and extent of erudi-
tion, which even then marked him as one of the
first literary characters of his age, he has added a
consummate knowledge in the commercial interest
of his country, formed by a long course of enlight-
ened and discriminating experience.

[18]   Sir, I should be inexcusable in coming after such
a person with any detail, if a great part of the
members who now fill the House had not the misfortune to be absent when he appeared at your bar.
Besides, Sir, I propose to take the matter at periods
of time somewhat different from his. There is, if
I mistake not, a point of view, from whence, if you
will look at this subject, it is impossible that it
should not make an impression upon you.

[19]   I have in my hand two accounts; one a comparative state of the export trade of England to its
colonies, as it stood in the year 1704, and as it

stood in the year 1772.   The other a state of the
export trade of this country to its colonies alone, as
it stood in 1772, compared with the whole trade
of England to all parts of the world (the colonies
included) in the year 1704.   They are from good
vouchers; the latter period from the accounts on
your table, the earlier from an original manuscript
of Davenant, who first established the inspector-
general's office, which has been ever since his time
so abundant a source of parliamentary information.

[20]   The export trade to the colonies consists of three
great branches.   The African, which, terminating
almost wholly in the colonies, must be put to the
account of their commerce; the West Indian; and
the North American.   All these are so interwoven,
that the attempt to separate them, would tear to
pieces the contexture of the whole; and if not
entirely destroy, would very much depreciate the
value of all the parts.   I therefore consider these
three denominations to be, what in effect they are,
one trade.

[21]   The trade to the colonies, taken on the export
side, at the beginning of this century, that is, in
the year 1704, stood thus:

Exports to North America, and the West Indies, ...	£483,265
To Africa, ...	86,665
	£569,930

[22]   In the year 1772, which I take as a middle year between the highest and lowest of those lately laid on your table, the account was as follows:

To North America, and the West
  Indies, ...   £4,791,734
To Africa, ...   866,398
To which, if you add the export
  trade from Scotland, which had
  in 1704 no existence,   . . .   364,000
                                   ─────────
                                  £6,022,132
                                   ─────────

[23]   From five hundred and odd thousand, it has grown to six millions. It has increased no less than twelve-fold. This is the state of the colony trade, as compared with itself at these two periods, within this century;—and this is matter for meditation. But this is not all. Examine my second account. See how the export trade to the colonies alone in 1772 stood in the other point of view, that is, as compared to the whole trade of England in 1704.

The whole export trade of England, including that to the colonies, in 1704, ...   £6,509,000
Export to the colonies alone, in
  1772, ...   6,024,000
                                  ─────────
              Difference,   £ 485,000
                                  ─────────

24]   The trade with America alone is now within less
than £500,000 of being equal to what this great
commercial nation, England, carried on at the
beginning of this century with the whole world!
If I had taken the largest year of those on your
table, it would rather have exceeded.   But, it will
be said, is not this American trade an unnatural
protuberance, that has drawn the juices from the
rest of the body? The reverse. It is the very
food that has nourished every other part into its
present magnitude. Our general trade has been
greatly augmented, and augmented more or less in
almost every part to which it ever extended; but
with this material difference, that of the six millions which in the beginning of the century constituted the whole mass of our export commerce, the
colony trade was but one-twelfth part; it is now
(as a part of sixteen millions) considerably more
than a third of the whole. This is the relative
proportion of the importance of the colonies at
these two periods: and all reasoning concerning
our mode of treating them must have this proportion as its basis, or it is a reasoning weak, rotten,
and sophistical.

25]   Mr. Speaker, I cannot prevail on myself to
hurry over this great consideration. It is good
for us to be here. We stand where we have
an immense view of what is, and what is past.
Clouds, indeed, and darkness rest upon the future.
Let us, however, before we descend from this noble

eminence, reflect that this growth of our national prosperity has happened within the short period of the life of man. It has happened within sixty-eight years. There are those alive whose memory might touch the two extremities. For instance, my Lord Bathurst might remember all the stages of the progress. He was in 1704 of an age at least to be made to comprehend such things. He was then old enough *acta parentum jam legere, et quæ sit poterit cognoscere virtus*[1]—Suppose, Sir, that the angel of this auspicious youth, foreseeing the many virtues, which made him one of the most amiable, as he is one of the most fortunate, men of his age, had opened to him in vision, that when, in the fourth generation, the third prince of the House of Brunswick had sat twelve years on the throne of that nation, which (by the happy issue of moderate and healing councils) was to be made Great Britain, he should see his son, Lord Chancellor of England, turn back the current of hereditary dignity to its fountain, and raise him to a higher rank of peerage, whilst he enriched the family with a new one—If amidst these bright and happy scenes of domestic honour and prosperity, that angel should have drawn up the curtain, and unfolded the rising glories of his country, and whilst he was gazing with admiration on the then

---

[1] To read about the deeds of his forefathers and to comprehend what manliness is.—Adapted from *Vergil. Eclogues, IV, 26, 27.*

commercial grandeur of England, the genius should point out to him a little speck, scarce visible in the mass of the national interest, a small seminal principle, rather than a formed body, and should tell him—"Young man, there is America—which at this day serves for little more than to amuse you with stories of savage men, and uncouth manners; yet shall, before you taste of death, show itself equal to the whole of that commerce which now attracts the envy of the world. Whatever England has been growing to by a progressive increase of improvement, brought in by varieties of people by succession of civilizing conquests and civilizing settlements in a series of seventeen hundred years, you shall see as much added to her by America in the course of a single life!" If this state of his country had been foretold to him, would it not require all the sanguine credulity of youth, and all the fervid glow of enthusiasm, to make him believe it? Fortunate man, he has lived to see it! Fortunate indeed, if he lives to see nothing that shall vary the prospect, and cloud the setting of his day!

26] Excuse, me, Sir, if turning from such thoughts I resume this comparative view once more. You have seen it on a large scale; look at it on a small one. I will point out to your attention a particular instance of it in the single province of Pennsylvania. In the year 1704, that province called for £11,459 in value of your commodities, native and foreign. This was the whole. What did it demand in 1772? Why, nearly fifty times as much; for in that year the export to Pennsylvania was £507,909, nearly equal to the export to all the colonies together in the first period.

[27] I choose, Sir, to enter into these minute and particular details because generalities, which in all other cases are apt to heighten and raise the subject, have here a tendency to sink it. When we speak of the commerce with our colonies, fiction lags after truth; invention is unfruitful, and imagination cold and barren.

[28] So far, Sir, as to the importance of the object in view of its commerce, as concerned in the exports from England. If I were to detail the imports, I could show how many enjoyments they procure, which deceive the burthen of life; how many materials which invigorate the springs of national industry, and extend and animate every part of our foreign and domestic commerce. This would be a curious subject indeed—but I must prescribe bounds to myself in a matter so vast and various.

[29] I pass therefore to the colonies in another point of view, their agriculture. This they have prosecuted with such a spirit, that, besides feeding plentifully their own growing multitude, their annual export of grain, comprehending rice, has some years ago exceeded a million in value. Of their last harvest, I am persuaded they will export

much more.   At the beginning of the century
some of these colonies imported corn from the
mother country.   For some time past, the Old
World has been fed from the New.   The scarcity
which you have felt would have been a desolating
famine, if this child of your old age, with a true
filial piety, with a Roman charity, had not put the
full breast of its youthful exuberance to the mouth
of its exhausted parent.

As to the wealth which the colonies have drawn
from the sea by their fisheries, you had all that
matter fully opened at your bar.   You surely
thought these acquisitions of value, for they
seemed even to excite your envy; and yet the
spirit by which that enterprising employment has
been exercised, ought rather, in my opinion, to
have raised your esteem and admiration.   And pray,
Sir, what in the world is equal to it?   Pass by the
other parts, and look at the manner in which the
people of New England have of late carried on
the whale fishery.   Whilst we follow them among
the tumbling mountains of ice, and behold them
penetrating into the deepest frozen recesses of
Hudson's Bay and Davis's Straits, whilst we are
looking for them beneath the arctic circle, we hear
that they have pierced into the opposite region of
polar cold, that they are at the antipodes, and
engaged under the frozen serpent of the south.
Falkland Island, which seemed too remote and
romantic an object for the grasp of national ambi-

tion, is but a stage and resting-place in the progress of their victorious industry. Nor is the equinoctial heat more discouraging to them, than the accumulated winter of both the poles. We know that whilst some of them draw the line and strike the harpoon on the coast of Africa, others run the longitude, and pursue their gigantic game along the coast of Brazil. No sea but what is vexed by their fisheries. No climate that is not witness to their toils. Neither the perseverance of Holland, nor the activity of France, nor the dexterous and firm sagacity of English enterprise, ever carried this most perilous mode of hard industry to the extent to which it has been pushed by this recent people; a people who are still, as it were, but in the gristle, and not yet hardened into the bone of manhood. When I contemplate these things; when I know that the colonies in general owe little or nothing to any care of ours, and that they are not squeezed into this happy form by the constraints of watchful and suspicious government, but that, through a wise and salutary neglect, a generous nature has been suffered to take her own way to perfection; when I reflect upon these effects, when I see how profitable they have been to us, I feel all the pride of power sink, and all presumption in the wisdom of human contrivances melt and die away within me. My rigour relents. I pardon something to the spirit of liberty.

[31] I am sensible, Sir, that all which I have asserted

in my detail, is admitted in the gross; but that quite a different conclusion is drawn from it. America, gentlemen say, is a noble object. It is an object well worth fighting for. Certainly it is, if fighting a people be the best way of gaining them. Gentlemen in this respect will be led to their choice of means by their complexions and their habits. Those who understand the military art, will of course have some predilection for it. Those who wield the thunder of the state, may have more confidence in the efficacy of arms. But I confess, possibly for want of this knowledge, my opinion is much more in favour of prudent management, than of force; considering force not as an odious, but a feeble instrument, for preserving a people so numerous, so active, so growing, so spirited as this, in a profitable and subordinate connexion with us.

2]   First, Sir, permit me to observe, that the use of force alone is but *temporary*. It may subdue for a moment; but it does not remove the necessity of subduing again: and a nation is not governed, which is perpetually to be conquered.

3]   My next objection is its *uncertainty*. Terror is not always the effect of force; and an armament is not a victory. If you do not succeed, you are without resource; for, conciliation failing, force remains; but, force failing, no further hope of reconciliation is left. Power and authority are sometimes bought by kindness; but they can never be begged as alms by an impoverished and defeated violence.

[34]   A further objection to force is, that you *impair the object* by your very endeavours to preserve it. The thing you fought for is not the thing which you recover; but depreciated, sunk, wasted, and consumed in the contest. Nothing less will content me, than *whole America*. I do not choose to consume its strength along with our own; because in all parts it is the British strength that I consume. I do not choose to be caught by a foreign enemy at the end of this exhausting conflict; and still less in the midst of it. I may escape; but I can make no insurance against such an event. Let me add, that I do not choose wholly to break the American spirit; because it is the spirit that has made the country.

[35]   Lastly, we have no sort of *experience* in favour of force as an instrument in the rule of our colonies. Their growth and their utility has been owing to methods altogether different. Our ancient indulgence has been said to be pursued to a fault. It may be so. But we know if feeling is evidence, that our fault was more tolerable than our attempt to mend it; and our sin far more salutary than our penitence.

[36]   These, Sir, are my reasons for not entertaining that high opinion of untried force, by which many gentlemen, for whose sentiments in other particulars I have great respect, seem to be so greatly

captivated.   But there is still behind a third consideration concerning this object, which serves to
determine my opinion on the sort of policy which
ought to be pursued in the management of America,
even more than its population and its commerce.
I mean its *temper and character*.

37]   In this character of the Americans, a love of
freedom is the predominating feature which marks
and distinguishes the whole: and as an ardent is
always a jealous affection, your colonies become
suspicious, restive, and untractable, whenever they
see the least attempt to wrest from them by force,
or shuffle from them by chicane, what they think
the only advantage worth living for.   This fierce
spirit of liberty is stronger in the English colonies
probably than in any other people of the earth; and
this from a great variety of powerful causes;
which, to understand the true temper of their
minds, and the direction which this spirit takes, it
will not be amiss to lay open somewhat more
largely.

38]   First, the people of the colonies are descendants
of Englishmen.   England, Sir, is a nation, which
still I hope respects, and formerly adored, her
freedom.   The colonists emigrated from you when
this part of your character was most predominant;
and they took this bias and direction the moment
they parted from your hands.   They are therefore
not only devoted to liberty, but to liberty according to English ideas, and on English principles.

Abstract liberty, like other mere abstractions, is not to be found. Liberty inheres in some sensible object; and every nation has formed to itself some favourite point, which by way of eminence becomes the criterion of their happiness. It happened, you know, Sir, that the great contests for freedom in this country were from the earliest times chiefly upon the question of taxing. Most of the contests in the ancient commonwealths turned primarily on the right of election of magistrates; or on the balance among the several orders of the state. The question of money was not with them so immediate. But in England it was otherwise. On this point of taxes the ablest pens, and most eloquent tongues, have been exercised; the greatest spirits have acted and suffered. In order to give the fullest satisfaction concerning the importance of this point, it was not only necessary for those who in argument defended the excellence of the English constitution, to insist on this privilege of granting money as a dry point of fact, and to prove, that the right had been acknowledged in ancient parchments, and blind usages, to reside in a certain body called a House of Commons. They went much farther; they attempted to prove, and they succeeded, that in theory it ought to be so, from the particular nature of a House of Commons, as an immediate representative of the people; whether the old records had delivered this oracle or not. They took infinite pains to inculcate, as a fundamental principle, that in all monarchies the people must in effect themselves, mediately or immediately, possess the power of granting their own money, or no shadow of liberty could subsist. The colonies draw from you, as with their life-blood, these ideas and principles. Their love of liberty, as with you, fixed and attached on this specific point of taxing. Liberty might be safe, or might be endangered, in twenty other particulars, without their being much pleased or alarmed. Here they felt its pulse; and as they found that beat, they thought themselves sick or sound. I do not say whether they were right or wrong in applying your general arguments to their own case. It is not easy indeed to make a monopoly of theorems and corollaries. The fact is, that they did thus apply those general arguments; and your mode of governing them, whether through lenity or indolence, through wisdom or mistake, confirmed them in the imagination, that they, as well as you, had an interest in these common principles.

9]   They were further confirmed in this pleasing error by the form of their provincial legislative assemblies. Their governments are popular in a high degree; some are merely popular; in all the popular representative is the most weighty; and this share of the people in their ordinary government never fails to inspire them with lofty sentiments, and with a strong aversion from whatever tends to deprive them of their chief importance.

[40] If anything were wanting to this necessary operation of the form of government, religion would have given it a complete effect. Religion, always a principle of energy, in this new people is no way worn out or impaired; and their mode of professing it is also one main cause of this free spirit. The people are Protestants; and of that kind which is the most adverse to all implicit submission of mind and opinion. This is a persuasion not only favourable to liberty, but built upon it. I do not think, Sir, that the reason of this averseness in the dissenting churches, from all that looks like absolute government, is so much to be sought in their religious tenets, as in their history. Every one knows that the Roman Catholic religion is at least coeval with most of the governments where it prevails; that it has generally gone hand in hand with them, and received great favour and every kind of support from authority. The Church of England too was formed from her cradle under the nursing care of regular government. But the dissenting interests have sprung up in direct opposition to all the ordinary powers of the world; and could justify that opposition only on a strong claim to natural liberty. Their very existence depended on the powerful and unremitted assertion of that claim. All Protestantism, even the most cold and passive, is a sort of dissent. But the religion most prevalent in our northern colonies is a refinement on the principle of resistance; it is the dissidence of

dissent, and the Protestantism of the Protestant religion. This religion, under a variety of denominations agreeing in nothing but in the communion of the spirit of liberty, is predominant in most of the northern provinces; where the Church of England, notwithstanding its legal rights, is in reality no more than a sort of private sect, not composing most probably the tenth of the people. The colonists left England when this spirit was high, and in the emigrants was the highest of all; and even that stream of foreigners, which has been constantly flowing into these colonies, has, for the greatest part, been composed of dissenters from the establishments of their several countries, and have brought with them a temper and character far from alien to that of the people with whom they mixed.

[41]   Sir, I can perceive by their manner, that some gentlemen object to the latitude of this description; because in the southern colonies the Church of England forms a large body, and has a regular establishment. It is certainly true. There is, however, a circumstance attending these colonies, which, in my opinion, fully counterbalances this difference, and makes the spirit of liberty still more high and haughty than in those to the northward. It is, that in Virginia and the Carolinas they have a vast multitude of slaves. Where this is the case in any part of the world, those who are free, are by far the most proud and jealous of their freedom.

Freedom is to them not only an enjoyment, but a kind of rank and privilege. Not seeing there, that freedom, as in countries where it is a common blessing, and as broad and general as the air, may be united with much abject toil, with great misery, with all the exterior of servitude, liberty looks, amongst them, like something that is more noble and liberal. I do not mean, Sir, to commend the superior morality of this sentiment, which has at least as much pride as virtue in it; but I cannot alter the nature of man. The fact is so; and these people of the southern colonies are much more strongly, and with a higher and more stubborn spirit, attached to liberty, than those to the northward. Such were all the ancient commonwealths; such were our Gothic ancestors; such in our days were the Poles; and such will be all masters of slaves, who are not slaves themselves. In such a people, the haughtiness of domination combines with the spirit of freedom, fortifies it, and renders it invincible.

[42]   Permit me, Sir, to add another circumstance in our colonies, which contributes no mean part towards the growth and effect of this untractable spirit. I mean their education. In no country perhaps in the world is the law so general a study. The profession itself is numerous and powerful; and in most provinces it takes the lead. The greater number of the deputies sent to the congress were lawyers. But all who read, and most

do read, endeavour to obtain some smattering in that science. I have been told by an eminent bookseller, that in no branch of his business, after tracts of popular devotion, were so many books as those on the law exported to the plantations. The colonists have now fallen into the way of printing them for their own use. I hear that they have sold nearly as many of Blackstone's Commentaries in America as in England. General Gage marks out this disposition very particularly in a letter on your table. He states, that all the people in his government are lawyers, or smatterers in law; and that in Boston they have been enabled, by successful chicane, wholly to evade many parts of one of your capital penal constitutions. The smartness of debate will say, that this knowledge ought to teach them more clearly the rights of legislature, their obligations to obedience, and the penalties of rebellion. All this is mighty well. But my honourable and learned friend on the floor, who condescends to mark what I say for animadversion, will disdain that ground. He has heard, as well as I, that when great honours and great emoluments do not win over this knowledge to the service of the state, it is a formidable adversary to government. If the spirit be not tamed and broken by these happy methods, it is stubborn and litigious. *Abeunt studia in mores.*[1]

---

[1] Pursuits (or studies) pass into character.—*Ovid, Heroides, XV, 83.* Compare *Bacon's Essay (Of Studies).*

This study renders men acute, inquisitive, dexterous, prompt in attack, ready in defence, full of resources. In other countries, the people, more simple, and of a less mercurial cast, judge of an ill principle in government only by an actual grievance; here they anticipate the evil, and judge of the pressure of the grievance by the badness of the principle. They augur misgovernment at a distance; and snuff the approach of tyranny in every tainted breeze.

[¶] The last cause of this disobedient spirit in the colonies is hardly less powerful than the rest, as it is not merely moral, but laid deep in the natural constitution of things. Three thousand miles of ocean lie between you and them. No contrivance can prevent the effect of this distance in weakening government. Seas roll, and months pass, between the order and the execution; and the want of a speedy explanation of a single point is enough to defeat a whole system. You have, indeed, winged ministers of vengeance, who carry your bolts in their pounces to the remotest verge of the sea. But there a power steps in, that limits the arrogance of raging passions and furious elements, and says, "So far shalt thou go, and no farther." Who are you, that should fret and rage, and bite the chains of nature?—Nothing worse happens to you than does to all nations who have extensive empire; and it happens in all the forms into which empire can be thrown. In large bodies, the circu-

lation of power must be less vigorous at the
extremities.   Nature has said it.   The Turk cannot govern Egypt, and Arabia, and Curdistan, as
he governs Thrace; nor has he the same dominion
in Crimea and Algiers, which he has at Brusa and
Smyrna.   Despotism itself is obliged to truck and
huckster.   The Sultan gets such obedience as he
can.   He governs with a loose rein, that he may
govern at all, and the whole of the force and
vigour of his authority in his centre is derived from
a prudent relaxation in all his borders.   Spain, in
her provinces, is, perhaps, not so well obeyed as
you are in yours.   She complies too; she submits;
she watches times.   This is the immutable condition, the eternal law, of extensive and detached
empire.

44]   Then, Sir, from these six capital sources; of
descent; of form of government; of religion in the
northern provinces; of manners in the southern;
of education; of the remoteness of situation from
the first mover of government; from all these
causes a fierce spirit of liberty has grown up.   It
has grown with the growth of the people in your
colonies, and increased with the increase of their
wealth; a spirit, that unhappily meeting with an
exercise of power in England, which, however law-
ful, is not reconcilable to any ideas of liberty, much
less with theirs, has kindled this flame that is ready
to consume us.

45]   I do not mean to commend either the spirit in

this excess, or the moral causes which produce it. Perhaps a more smooth and accommodating spirit of freedom in them would be more acceptable to us. Perhaps ideas of liberty might be desired, more reconcilable with an arbitrary and boundless authority. Perhaps we might wish the colonists to be persuaded, that their liberty is more secure when held in trust for them by us (as their guardians during a perpetual minority) than with any part of it in their own hands. The question is, not whether their spirit deserves praise or blame, but—what, in the name of God, shall we do with it? You have before you the object, such as it is, with all its glories, with all its imperfections on its head. You see the magnitude; the importance; the temper; the habits; the disorders. By all these considerations we are strongly urged to determine something concerning it. We are called upon to fix some rule and line for our future conduct, which may give a little stability to our politics, and prevent the return of such unhappy deliberations as the present. Every such return will bring the matter before us in a still more untractable form. For, what astonishing and incredible things have we not seen already! What monsters have not been generated from this unnatural contention! Whilst every principle of authority and resistance has been pushed, upon both sides, as far as it would go, there is nothing so solid and certain, either in reasoning or in practice, that has not

ьeen shaken. Until very lately, all authority in
America seemed to be nothing but an emanation
from yours. Even the popular part of the colony
constitution derived all its activity, and its first
vital movement, from the pleasure of the crown.
We thought, Sir, that the utmost which the discontented colonists could do, was to disturb
authority; we never dreamt they could of themselves supply it; knowing in general what an
operose business it is to establish a government
absolutely new. But having, for our purposes in
this contention, resolved, that none but an obedient
assembly should sit; the humours of the people
there, finding all passage through the legal chan-
nel stopped, with great violence broke out another
way. Some provinces have tried their experiment, as we have tried ours; and theirs has
succeeded. They have formed a government
sufficient for its purposes, without the bustle of a
revolution, or the troublesome formality of an
election. Evident necessity, and tacit consent,
have done the business in an instant. So well
they have done it, that Lord Dunmore (the
account is among the fragments on your table)
tells you, that the new institution is infinitely
better obeyed than the ancient government ever
was in its most fortunate periods. Obedience is
what makes government, and not the names by
which it is called; not the name of governor, as
formerly, or committee, as at present. This new

government has originated directly from the
people; and was not transmitted through any of
the ordinary artificial media of a positive constitution. It was not a manufacture ready formed, and
transmitted to them in that condition from England. The evil arising from hence is this; that
the colonists having once found the possibility of
enjoying the advantages of order in the midst of a
struggle for liberty, such struggles will not hence-
forward seem so terrible to the settled and sober
part of mankind as they had appeared before the
trial.

[46]   Pursuing the same plan of punishing by the
denial of the exercise of government to still greater
lengths, we wholly abrogated the ancient government of Massachusetts. We were confident that
the first feeling, if not the very prospect of anarchy,
would instantly enforce a complete submission.
The experiment was tried. A new, strange, unex-
pected face of things appeared. Anarchy is found
tolerable. A vast province has now subsisted, and
subsisted in a considerable degree of health and
vigour, for near a twelvemonth, without governor,
without public council, without judges, without
executive magistrates. How long it will continue
in this state, or what may arise out of this unheard-
of situation, how can the wisest of us conjecture?
Our late experience has taught us that many of
those fundamental principles, formerly believed
infallible, are either not of the importance they

were imagined to be; or that we have not at all
adverted to some other far more important and far
more powerful principles, which entirely overrule
those we had considered as omnipotent.   I am
much against any further experiments, which tend
to put to the proof any more of these allowed
opinions, which contribute so much to the public
tranquillity.   In effect, we suffer as much at home
by this loosening of all ties, and this concussion of
all established opinions, as we do abroad.   For, in
order to prove that the Americans have no right to
their liberties, we are every day endeavouring to
subvert the maxims which preserve the whole spirit
of our own.   To prove that the Americans ought
not to be free, we are obliged to depreciate the
value of freedom itself; and we never seem to gain
a paltry advantage over them in debate, without
attacking some of those principles, or deriding
some of those feelings, for which our ancestors have
shed their blood.

[47]   But, Sir, in wishing to put an end to pernicious
experiments, I do not mean to preclude the fullest
inquiry.   Far from it.   Far from deciding on a
sudden or partial view, I would patiently go round
and round the subject, and survey it minutely in
every possible aspect.   Sir, if I were capable of
engaging you to an equal attention, I would state,
that, as far as I am capable of discerning, there
are but three ways of proceeding relative to this
stubborn spirit, which prevails in your colonies,

and disturbs your government. These are—To change that spirit, as inconvenient, by removing the causes. To prosecute it as criminal. Or, to comply with it as necessary. I would not be guilty of an imperfect enumeration; I can think of but these three. Another has indeed been started, that of giving up the colonies; but it met so slight a reception, that I do not think myself obliged to dwell a great while upon it. It is nothing but a little sally of anger, like the frowardness of peevish children, who, when they cannot get all they would have, are resolved to take nothing.

[48]   The first of these plans, to change the spirit as inconvenient, by removing the causes, I think is the most like a systematic proceeding. It is radical in its principle; but it is attended with great difficulties, some of them little short, as I conceive, of impossibilities. This will appear by examining into the plans which have been proposed.

[49]   As the growing population in the colonies is evidently one cause of their resistance, it was last session mentioned in both Houses, by men of weight, and received not without applause, that in order to check this evil, it would be proper for the crown to make no further grants of land. But to this scheme there are two objections. The first, that there is already so much unsettled land in private hands, as to afford room for an immense future population, although the crown not only withheld its grants, but annihilated its soil. If

this be the case, then the only effect of this avarice of desolation, this hoarding of a royal wilderness, would be to raise the value of the possessions in the hands of the great private monopolists, without any adequate check to the growing and alarming mischief of population.

0]   But if you stopped your grants, what would be the consequence? The people would occupy without grants. They have already so occupied in many places. You cannot station garrisons in every part of these deserts. If you drive the people from one place, they will carry on their annual tillage, and remove with their flocks and herds to another. Many of the people in the back settlements are already little attached to particular situations. Already they have topped the Appalachian mountains. From thence they behold before them an immense plain, one vast, rich, level meadow; a square of five hundred miles. Over this they would wander without a possibility of restraint; they would change their manners with the habits of their life; would soon forget a government by which they were disowned; would become hordes of English Tartars; and pouring down upon your unfortified frontiers a fierce and irresistible cavalry, become masters of your governors and your counsellors, your collectors and comptrollers, and of all the slaves that adhered to them. Such would, and, in no long time, must be, the effect of attempting to forbid as a crime, and to suppress as an evil, the command and blessing of Providence, "Increase and multiply." Such would be the happy result of an endeavour to keep as a lair of wild beasts, that earth, which God, by an express charter, has given to the children of men. Far different, and surely much wiser, has been our policy hitherto. Hitherto we have invited our people, by every kind of bounty, to fixed establishments. We have invited the husbandman to look to authority for his title. We have taught him piously to believe in the mysterious virtue of wax and parchment. We have thrown each tract of land, as it was peopled, into districts; that the ruling power should never be wholly out of sight. We have settled all we could; and we have carefully attended every settlement with government.

[51]   Adhering, Sir, as I do, to this policy, as well as for the reasons I have just given, I think this new project of hedging-in population to be neither prudent nor practicable.

[52]   To impoverish the colonies in general, and in particular to arrest the noble course of their marine enterprises, would be a more easy task. I freely confess it. We have shown a disposition to a system of this kind; a disposition even to continue the restraint after the offence; looking on ourselves as rivals to our colonies, and persuaded that of course we must gain all that they shall lose. Much mischief we may certainly do. The power

inadequate to all other things is often more than sufficient for this. I do not look on the direct and immediate power of the colonies to resist our violence as very formidable. In this, however, I may be mistaken. But when I consider, that we have colonies for no purpose but to be serviceable to us, it seems to my poor understanding a little preposterous, to make them unserviceable, in order to keep them obedient. It is, in truth, nothing more than the old, and, as I thought, exploded problem of tyranny, which proposes to beggar its subjects into submission. But remember, when you have completed your system of impoverishment, that nature still proceeds in her ordinary course; that discontent will increase with misery; and that there are critical moments in the fortune of all states, when they who are too weak to contribute to your prosperity, may be strong enough to complete your ruin. *Spoliatis arma supersunt.*[1]

[53] The temper and character which prevail in our colonies are, I am afraid, unalterable by any human art. We cannot, I fear, falsify the pedigree of this fierce people, and persuade them that they are not sprung from a nation in whose veins the blood of freedom circulates. The language in which they would hear you tell them this tale would detect the imposition; your speech would

---

[1] Those who have been despoiled may still resort to arms.—*Juvenal, Satires, VIII, 124.*

betray you. An Englishman is the unfittest person on earth to argue another Englishman into slavery.

[54] I think it is nearly as little in our power to change their republican religion, as their free descent; or to substitute the Roman Catholic, as a penalty; or the Church of England, as an improvement. The mode of inquisition and dragooning is going out of fashion in the Old World; and I should not confide much to their efficacy in the New. The education of the Americans is also on the same unalterable bottom with their religion. You cannot persuade them to burn their books of curious science; to banish their lawyers from their courts of laws; or to quench the lights of their assemblies, by refusing to choose those persons who are best read in their privileges. It would be no less impracticable to think of wholly annihilating the popular assemblies, in which these lawyers sit. The army, by which we must govern in their place, would be far more chargeable to us; not quite so effectual; and perhaps, in the end, full as difficult to be kept in obedience.

[55] With regard to the high aristocratic spirit of Virginia and the southern colonies, it has been proposed I know to reduce it, by declaring a general enfranchisement of their slaves. This project has had its advocates and panegyrists; yet I never could argue myself into any opinion of it. Slaves are often much attached to their masters. . A

general wild offer of liberty would not always be accepted. History furnishes few instances of it. It is sometimes as hard to persuade slaves to be free, as it is to compel freemen to be slaves; and in this auspicious scheme, we should have both these pleasing tasks on our hands at once. But when we talk of enfranchisement, do we not perceive that the American master may enfranchise too; and arm servile hands in defence of freedom? A measure to which other people have had recourse more than once, and not without success, in a desperate situation of their affairs.

56]   Slaves as these unfortunate black people are, and dull as all men are from slavery, must they not a little suspect the offer of freedom from that very nation, which has sold them to their present masters? from that nation one of whose causes of quarrel with those masters is their refusal to deal any more in that inhuman traffic? An offer of freedom from England would come rather oddly, shipped to them in an African vessel, which is refused an entry into the ports of Virginia or Carolina, with a cargo of three hundred Angola negroes. It would be curious to see the Guinea captain attempting at the same instant to publish his proclamation of liberty, and to advertise his sale of slaves.

57]   But let us suppose all these moral difficulties got over. The ocean remains. You cannot pump this dry; and as long as it continues in its present bed, so long all the causes which weaken authority by distance will continue.

> *Ye gods, annihilate but space and time,*
> *And make two lovers happy!*

—was a pious and passionate prayer;—but just as reasonable, as many of the serious wishes of very grave and solemn politicians.

[58]   If then, Sir, it seems almost desperate to think of any alterative course, for changing the moral causes (and not quite easy to remove the natural) which produce prejudices irreconcilable to the late exercise of our authority; but that the spirit infallibly will continue; and, continuing, will produce such effects as now embarrass us; the second mode under consideration is, to prosecute that spirit in its overt acts, as *criminal*.

[59]   At this proposition I must pause a moment. The thing seems a great deal too big for my ideas of jurisprudence.   It should seem to my way of conceiving such matters, that there is a very wide difference in reason and policy, between the mode of proceeding on their regular conduct of scattered individuals, or even of bands of men, who disturb order within the state, and the civil dissensions which may, from time to time, on great questions, agitate the several communities which compose a great empire.   It looks to me to be narrow and pedantic, to apply the ordinary ideas of criminal justice to this great public contest.   I do not know

the method of drawing up an indictment against a whole people. I cannot insult and ridicule the feelings of millions of my fellow-creatures, as Sir Edward Coke insulted one excellent individual (Sir Walter Raleigh) at the bar. I hope I am not ripe to pass sentence on the gravest public bodies, intrusted with magistracies of great authority and dignity, and charged with the safety of their fellow-citizens, upon the very same title that I am. I really think, that for wise men this is not judicious; for sober men, not decent; for minds tinctured with humanity, not mild and merciful.

[60]   Perhaps, Sir, I am mistaken in my idea of an empire, as distinguished from a single state or kingdom. But my idea of it is this; that an empire is the aggregate of many states under one common head; whether this head be a monarch, or a presiding republic. It does, in such constitutions, frequently happen (and nothing but the dismal, cold, dead uniformity of servitude can prevent its happening) that the subordinate parts have many local privileges and immunities. Between these privileges and the supreme common authority the line may be extremely nice. Of course disputes, often, too, very bitter disputes, and much ill blood, will arise, but though every privilege is an exemption (in the case) from the ordinary exercise of the supreme authority, it is no denial of it. The claim of a privilege seems rather, *ex vi termini*, to imply a superior power. For to

talk of the privileges of a state, or of a person, who has no superior, is hardly any better than speaking nonsense.   Now, in such unfortunate quarrels among the component parts of a great political union of communities, I can scarcely conceive anything more completely imprudent, than for the head of the empire to insist, that, if any privilege is pleaded against his will, or his acts, his whole authority is denied; instantly to proclaim rebellion, to beat to arms, and to put the offending provinces under the ban.   Will not this, Sir, very soon teach the provinces to make no distinctions on their part?   Will it not teach them that the government, against which a claim of liberty is tantamount to high treason, is a government to which submission is equivalent to slavery?   It may not always be quite convenient to impress dependent communities with such an idea.

[61]   We are indeed, in all disputes with the colonies, by the necessity of things, the judge.   It is true, Sir.   But I confess, that the character of judge in my own cause is a thing that frightens me. Instead of filling me with pride, I am exceedingly humbled by it.   I cannot proceed with a stern, assured, judicial confidence, until I find myself in something more like a judicial character.   I must have these hesitations as long as I am compelled to recollect, that, in my little reading upon such contests as these, the sense of mankind has, at least, as often decided against the superior as the

subordinate power. Sir, let me add too, that the
opinion of my having some abstract right in my
favour, would not put me much at my ease in
passing sentence; unless I could be sure, that there
were no rights which, in their exercise under certain circumstances, were not the most odious of all
wrongs, and the most vexatious of all injustice.
Sir, these considerations have great weight with
me, when I find things so circumstanced, that I
see the same party, at once a civil litigant against
me in point of right, and a culprit before me; while
I sit as a criminal judge, on acts of his, whose
moral quality is to be decided upon the merits of
that very litigation. Men are every now and then
put; by the complexity of human affairs, into
strange situations; but justice is the same, let the
judge be in what situation he will.

[62]   There is, Sir, also a circumstance which con-
vinces me, that this mode of criminal proceeding
is not (at least in the present stage of our contest)
altogether expedient; which is nothing less than
the conduct of those very persons who have seemed
to adopt that mode, by lately declaring a rebellion
in Massachusetts Bay, as they had formerly
addressed to have traitors brought hither, under an
act of Henry the Eighth, for trial. For though
rebellion is declared, it is not proceeded against as
such; nor have any steps been taken towards the
apprehension or conviction of any individual
offender, either on our late or our former address;

but modes of public coercion have been adopted, and such as have much more resemblance to a sort of qualified hostility towards an independent power than the punishment of rebellious subjects. All this seems rather inconsistent; but it shows how difficult it is to apply these juridical ideas to our present case.

[63] In this situation, let us seriously and coolly ponder. What is it we have got by all our menaces, which have been many and ferocious? What advantage have we derived from the penal laws we have passed, and which, for the time, have been severe and numerous? What advances have we made towards our object, by the sending of a force, which, by land and sea, is no contemptible strength? Has the disorder abated? Nothing less.—When I see things in this situation, after such confident hopes, bold promises, and active exertions, I cannot, for my life, avoid a suspicion, that the plan itself is not correctly right.

[64] If then the removal of the causes of this spirit of American liberty be, for the greater part, or rather entirely, impracticable; if the ideas of criminal process be inapplicable, or if applicable, are in the highest degree inexpedient; what way yet remains? No way is open, but the third and last—to comply with the American spirit as necessary; or, if you please, to submit to it as a necessary evil.

[65] If we adopt this mode; if we mean to conciliate and concede; let us see of what nature the con-

cession ought to be: to ascertain the nature of our
concession, we must look at their complaint. The
colonies complain, that they have not the characteristic mark and seal of British freedom. They
complain, that they are taxed in a parliament in
which they are not represented. If you mean to
satisfy them at all, you must satisfy them with regard to this complaint. If you mean to please any
people, you must give them the boon which they
ask; not what you may think better for them, but
of a kind totally different. Such an act may be a
wise regulation, but it is no concession: whereas
our present theme is the mode of giving satisfaction.

[66] Sir, I think you must perceive, that I am resolved
this day to have nothing at all to do with the
question of the right of taxation. Some gentlemen startle—but it is true; I put it totally out of
the question. It is less than nothing in my consideration. I do not indeed wonder, nor will you,
Sir, that gentlemen of profound learning are fond
of displaying it on this profound subject. But my
consideration is narrow, confined, and wholly
limited to the policy of the question. I do not
examine, whether the giving away a man's money
be a power excepted and reserved out of the general trust of government; and how far all mankind,
in all forms of polity, are entitled to an exercise of
that right by the charter of nature. Or whether,
on the contrary, a right of taxation is necessarily
involved in the general principle of legislation, and

inseparable from the ordinary supreme power.
These are deep questions, where great names
militate against each other; where reason is perplexed; and an appeal to authorities only thickens
the confusion. For high and reverend authorities
lift up their heads on both sides; and there is no
sure footing in the middle. This point is the

> *great Serbonian bog,*
> *Betwixt Damiata and Mount Casius old,*
> *Where armies whole have sunk.*

I do not intend to be overwhelmed in that bog,
though in such respectable company. The question
with me is, not whether you have a right to render
your people miserable; but whether it is not your
interest to make them happy. It is not, what a
lawyer tells me I *may* do; but what humanity, reason, and justice tell me I ought to do. Is a politic
act the worse for being a generous one? Is no concession proper, but that which is made from your
want of right to keep what you grant? Or does it
lessen the grace or dignity of relaxing in the exercise
of an odious claim, because you have your evidence-
room full of titles, and your magazines stuffed with
arms to enforce them? What signify all those
titles, and all those arms? Of what avail are they,
when the reason of the thing tells me, that the
assertion of my title is the loss of my suit; and
that I could do nothing but wound myself by the
use of my own weapons?

37]   Such is steadfastly my opinion of the absolute
necessity of keeping up the concord of this empire
by a unity of spirit, though in a diversity of oper-
ations, that, if I were sure the colonists had, at
their leaving this country, sealed a regular compact
of servitude; that they had solemnly abjured all
the rights of citizens; that they had made a vow to
renounce all ideas of liberty for them and their
posterity to all generations; yet I should hold
myself obliged to conform to the temper I found
universally prevalent in my own day, and to govern
two millions of men, impatient of servitude, on the
principles of freedom.   I am not determining a
point of law; I am restoring tranquillity; and the
general character and situation of a people must
determine what sort of government is fitted for
them.   That point nothing else can or ought to
determine.

38]   My idea therefore, without considering whether
we yield as matter of right, or grant as matter of
favour, is *to admit the people of our colonies into
an interest in the constitution;* and, by recording
that admission in the journals of parliament, to
give them as strong an assurance as the nature of
the thing will admit, that we mean for ever to
adhere to that solemn declaration of systematic
indulgence.

39]   Some years ago, the repeal of a revenue act,
upon its understood principle, might have served
to show, that we intended an unconditional abate-

ment of the exercise of a taxing power. Such a measure was then sufficient to remove all suspicion, and to give perfect content. But unfortunate events, since that time, may make something further necessary; and not more necessary for the satisfaction of the colonies, than for the dignity and consistency of our own future proceedings.

[70]   I have taken a very incorrect measure of the disposition of the House, if this proposal in itself would be received with dislike. I think, Sir, I have few American financiers. But our misfortune is, we are too acute; we are too exquisite in our conjectures of the future, for men oppressed with such great and present evils. The more moderate among the opposers of parliamentary concession freely confess, that they hope no good from taxation; but they apprehend the colonists have further views; and if this point were conceded, they would instantly attack the trade laws. These gentlemen are convinced, that this was the intention from the beginning; and the quarrel of the Americans with taxation was no more than a cloak and cover to this design. Such has been the language even of a gentleman of real moderation, and of a natural temper well adjusted to fair and equal government. I am, however, Sir, not a little surprised at this kind of discourse, whenever I hear it; and I am the more surprised, on account of the arguments which I constantly find in company with it, and

which are often urged from the same mouths, and on the same day.

1] For instance, when we allege that it is against reason to tax a people under so many restraints in trade as the Americans, the noble lord in the blue riband shall tell you, that the restraints on trade are futile and useless; of no advantage to us, and of no burthen to those on whom they are imposed; that the trade to America is not secured by the acts of navigation, but by the natural and irresistible advantage of a commercial preference.

2] Such is the merit of the trade laws in this posture of the debate. But when strong internal circumstances are urged against the taxes; when the scheme is dissected; when experience and the nature of things are brought to prove, and do prove, the utter impossibility of obtaining an effective revenue from the colonies; when these things are pressed, or rather press themselves, so as to drive the advocates of colony taxes to a clear admission of the futility of the scheme; then, Sir, the sleeping trade laws revive from their trance; and this useless taxation is to be kept sacred, not for its own sake, but as a counter-guard and security of the laws of trade.

3] Then, Sir, you keep up revenue laws which are mischievous, in order to preserve trade laws that are useless. Such is the wisdom of our plan in both its members. They are separately given up as of no value; and yet one is always to be defended for the sake of the other. But I cannot agree with the noble lord, nor with the pamphlet from whence he seems to have borrowed these ideas, concerning the inutility of the trade laws. For, without idolizing them, I am sure they are still, in many ways, of great use to us: and in former times they have been of the greatest. They do confine, and they do greatly narrow, the market for the Americans. But my perfect conviction of this does not help me in the least to discern how the revenue laws form any security whatsoever to the commercial regulations; or that these commercial regulations are the true ground of the quarrel; or that the giving way, in any one instance, of authority, is to lose all that may remain unconceded.

[74] One fact is clear and indisputable. The public and avowed origin of this quarrel was on taxation. This quarrel has indeed brought on new disputes on new questions; but certainly the least bitter, and the fewest of all, on the trade laws. To judge which of the two be the real, radical cause of quarrel, we have to see whether the commercial dispute did, in order of time, precede the dispute on taxation? There is not a shadow of evidence for it. Next, to enable us to judge whether at this moment a dislike to the trade laws be the real cause of quarrel, it is absolutely necessary to put the taxes out of the question by a repeal. See how the Americans act in this position, and then you

will be able to discern correctly what is the true object of the controversy, or whether any controversy at all will remain. Unless you consent to remove this cause of difference, it is impossible, with decency, to assert that the dispute is not upon what it is avowed to be. And I would, Sir, recommend to your serious consideration, whether it be prudent to form a rule for punishing people, not on their own acts, but on your conjectures? Surely it is preposterous at the very best. It is not justifying your anger, by their misconduct; but it is converting your ill-will into their delinquency.

75] But the colonies will go further.—Alas! alas! when will this speculating against fact and reason end?—What will quiet these panic fears which we entertain of the hostile effect of a conciliatory conduct? Is it true, that no case can exist, in which it is proper for the sovereign to accede to the desires of his discontented subjects? Is there anything peculiar in this case, to make a rule for itself? Is all authority of course lost, when it is not pushed to the extreme? Is it a certain maxim, that the fewer causes of dissatisfaction are left by government, the more the subject will be inclined to resist and rebel?

76] All these objections being in fact no more than suspicions, conjectures, divinations, formed in defiance of fact and experience; they did not, Sir, discourage me from entertaining the idea of a conciliatory concession, founded on the principles which I have just stated.

[77]   In forming a plan for this purpose, I endeavoured to put myself in that frame of mind which was the most natural, and the most reasonable; and which was certainly the most probable means of securing me from all error. I set out with a perfect distrust of my own abilities; a total renunciation of every speculation of my own; and with a profound reverence for the wisdom of our ancestors, who have left us the inheritance of so happy a constitution, and so flourishing an empire, and what is a thousand times more valuable, the treasury of the maxims and principles which formed the one, and obtained the other.

[78]   During the reigns of the kings of Spain of the Austrian family, whenever they were at a loss in the Spanish councils, it was common for their statesmen to say, that they ought to consult the genius of Philip the Second. The genius of Philip the Second might mislead them; and the issue of their affairs showed, that they had not chosen the most perfect standard. But, Sir, I am sure that I shall not be misled, when, in a case of constitutional difficulty, I consult the genius of the English constitution. Consulting at that oracle (it was with all due humility and piety) I found four capital examples in a similar case before me; those of Ireland, Wales, Chester, and Durham.

9] Ireland, before the English conquest, though never governed by a despotic power, had no parliament. How far the English parliament itself was at that time modelled according to the present form, is disputed among antiquarians. But we have all the reason in the world to be assured that a form of parliament, such as England then enjoyed, she instantly communicated to Ireland; and we are equally sure that almost every successive improvement in constitutional liberty, as fast as it was made here, was transmitted thither. The feudal baronage, and the feudal knighthood, the roots of our primitive constitution, were early transplanted into that soil; and grew and flourished there. Magna Charta, if it did not give us originally the House of Commons, gave us at least a House of Commons of weight and consequence. But your ancestors did not churlishly sit down alone to the feast of Magna Charta. Ireland was made immediately a partaker. This benefit of English laws and liberties, I confess, was not at first extended to *all* Ireland. Mark the consequence, English authority and English liberties had exactly the same boundaries. Your standard could never be advanced an inch before your privileges. Sir John Davis shows beyond a doubt, that the refusal of a general communication of these rights was the true cause why Ireland was five hundred years in subduing; and after the vain projects of a military government, attempted in the reign of

Queen Elizabeth, it was soon discovered, that nothing could make that country English, in civility and allegiance, but your laws and your forms of legislature. It was not English arms, but the English constitution, that conquered Ireland. From that time, Ireland has ever had a general parliament, as she had before a partial parliament. You changed the people; you altered the religion; but you never touched the form or the vital substance of free government in that kingdom. You deposed kings; you restored them; you altered the succession to theirs, as well as to your own crown; but you never altered their constitution; the principle of which was respected by usurpation; restored with the restoration of monarchy, and established, I trust, for ever, by the glorious Revolution. This has made Ireland the great and flourishing kingdom that it is; and from a disgrace and a burthen intolerable to this nation, has rendered her a principal part of our strength and ornament. This country cannot be said to have ever formally taxed her. The irregular things done in the confusion of mighty troubles, and on the hinge of great revolutions, even if all were done that is said to have been done, form no example. If they have any effect in argument, they make an exception to prove the rule. None of your own liberties could stand a moment if the casual deviations from them, at such times, were suffered to be used as proofs of their nullity. By the lucrative amount of such casual breaches in the constitution, judge what the stated and fixed rule of supply has been in that kingdom. Your Irish pensioners would starve if they had no other fund to live on than taxes granted by English authority. Turn your eyes to those popular grants from whence all your great supplies are come; and learn to respect that only source of public wealth in the British empire.

[20] My next example is Wales. This country was said to be reduced by Henry the Third. It was said more truly to be so by Edward the First. But though then conquered, it was not looked upon as any part of the realm of England. Its old constitution, whatever that might have been, was destroyed; and no good one was substituted in its place. The care of that tract was put into the hands of lords marchers—a form of government of a very singular kind; a strange heterogeneous monster, something between hostility and government; perhaps it has a sort of resemblance, according to the modes of those times, to that of commander-in-chief at present, to whom all civil power is granted as secondary. The manners of the Welsh nation followed the genius of the government; the people were ferocious, restive, savage, and uncultivated; sometimes composed, never pacified. Wales, within itself, was in perpetual disorder; and it kept the frontier of England in perpetual alarm. Benefits from it to the state

there were none. Wales was only known to England by incursion and invasion.

[81] Sir, during that state of things, parliament was not idle. They attempted to subdue the fierce spirit of the Welsh by all sorts of rigorous laws. They prohibited by statute the sending all sorts of arms into Wales, as you prohibit by proclamation (with something more of doubt on the legality) the sending arms to America. They disarmed the Welsh by statute, as you attempted (but still with more question on the legality) to disarm New England by an instruction. They made an act to drag offenders from Wales into England for trial, as you have done (but with more hardship) with regard to America. By another act, where one of the parties was an Englishman, they ordained, that his trial should be always by English. They made acts to restrain trade, as you do; and they prevented the Welsh from the use of fairs and markets, as you do the Americans from fisheries and foreign ports. In short, when the statute book was not quite so much swelled as it is now, you find no less than fifteen acts of penal regulation on the subject of Wales.

[82] Here we rub our hands—A fine body of precedents for the authority of parliament and the use of it!—I admit it fully; and pray add likewise to these precedents, that all the while, Wales rid this kingdom like an *incubus;* that it was an unprofitable and oppressive burthen; and that an

Englishman travelling in that country could not go six yards from the high road without being murdered.

The march of the human mind is slow.   Sir, it was not, until after two hundred years, discovered, that, by an eternal law, Providence had decreed vexation to violence, and poverty to rapine.   Your ancestors did however at length open their eyes to the ill husbandry of injustice.   They found that the tyranny of a free people could of all tyrannies the least be endured; and that laws made against a whole nation were not the most effectual methods for securing its obedience. Accordingly, in the twenty-seventh year of Henry VIII. the course was entirely altered.   With a preamble stating the entire and perfect rights of the crown of England, it gave to the Welsh all the rights and privileges of English subjects.   A political order was established; the military power gave way to the civil; the marches were turned into counties.   But that a nation should have a right to English liberties, and yet no share at all in the fundamental security of these liberties—the grant of their own property—seemed a thing so incongruous, that, eight years after, that is, in the thirty-fifth of that reign, a complete and not ill-proportioned representation by counties and boroughs was bestowed upon Wales, by act of parliament.   From that moment, as by a charm, the tumults subsided, obedience was restored, peace.

order, and civilization followed in the train of
liberty.—When the day-star of the English constitution had arisen in their hearts, all was harmony
within and without—

> —Simul alba nautis
>   Stella refulsit
> Defluit saxis agitatus humor;
> Concidunt venti, fugiúntque nubes,
> Et minax (quòd sic voluere) ponto
>   Unda recumbit.[1]

[84] The very same year the county palatine of
Chester received the same relief from its oppres-
sions, and the same remedy to its disorders.
Before this time Chester was little less distempered
than Wales. The inhabitants, without rights themselves, were the fittest to destroy the rights of
others; and from thence Richard II. drew the
standing army of archers, with which for a time
he oppressed England. The people of Chester
applied to parliament in a petition penned as I
shall read to you:

[85] "To the king our sovereign lord, in most humble
wise shown unto your excellent Majesty, the
inhabitants of your Grace's county palatine of
Chester; That where the said county palatine of

---

[1] As soon as the bright star has shone upon the sailors,
the troubled water recedes from the rocks, the winds
die away, the clouds scatter, and, because they [Castor
and Pollux] have so willed, the threatening wave sub-
sides upon the deep.—*Horace, Odes, I. xii, 27-32.*

Chester is and hath been always hitherto exempt, excluded and separated out and from your high court of parliament, to have any knights and burgesses within the said court; by reason whereof the said inhabitants have hitherto sustained manifold disherisons, losses, and damages, as well in their lands, goods, and bodies, as in the good, civil, and politic governance and maintenance of the commonwealth of their said country: (2) And forasmuch as the said inhabitants have always hitherto been bound by the acts and statutes made and ordained by your said Highness, and your most noble progenitors, by authority of the said court, as far forth as other counties, cities, and boroughs have been, that have had their knights and burgesses within your said court of parliament, and yet have had neither knight ne burgess there for the said county palatine; the said inhabitants, for lack thereof, have been oftentimes touched and grieved with acts and statutes made within the said court, as well derogatory unto the most ancient jurisdictions, liberties, and privileges of your said county palatine, as prejudicial unto the commonwealth, quietness, rest, and peace of your Grace's most bounden subjects inhabiting within the same."

86]   What did parliament with this audacious address? —Reject it as a libel? Treat it as an affront to government? Spurn it as a derogation from the rights of legislature? Did they toss it over the

table? Did they burn it by the hands of the
common hangman? They took the petition of
grievance, all rugged as it was, without softening
or temperament, unpurged of the original bitter-
ness and indignation of complaint; they made it the
very preamble to their act of redress; and consecrated its principle to all ages in the sanctuary of
legislation.

[87]   Here is my third example. It was attended
with the success of the two former. Chester,
civilized as well as Wales, has demonstrated that
freedom, and not servitude, is the cure of anarchy;
as religion, and not atheism, is the true remedy
for superstition. Sir, this pattern of Chester was
followed in the reign of Charles II. with regard to
the county palatine of Durham, which is my
fourth example. This county had long lain out
of the pale of free legislation. So scrupulously
was the example of Chester followed, that the
style of the preamble is nearly the same with that
of the Chester act; and, without affecting the
abstract extent of the authority of parliament, it
recognises the equity of not suffering any considerable district, in which the British subjects may act
as a body, to be taxed without their own voice in
the grant.

[88]   Now if the doctrines of policy contained in
these preambles, and the force of these examples
in the acts of parliament, avail anything, what
can be said against applying them with regard to

America? Are not the people of America as much
Englishmen as the Welsh? The preamble of the
act of Henry VIII. says, the Welsh speak a
language no way resembling that of his Majesty's
English subjects. Are the Americans not as
numerous? If we may trust the learned and
accurate Judge Barrington's account of North
Wales, and take that as a standard to measure the
rest, there is no comparison. The people cannot
amount to above 200,000; not a tenth part of the
number in the colonies. Is America in rebellion?
Wales was hardly ever free from it. Have you
attempted to govern America by penal statutes?
You made fifteen for Wales. But your legislative
authority is perfect with regard to America; was
it less perfect in Wales, Chester, and Durham?
But America is virtually represented. What!
does the electric force of virtual representation
more easily pass over the Atlantic, than pervade
Wales, which lies in your neighbourhood; or than
Chester and Durham, surrounded by abundance of
representation that is actual and palpable? But,
Sir, your ancestors thought this sort of virtual
representation, however ample, to be totally
insufficient for the freedom of the inhabitants of
territories that are so near, and comparatively so
inconsiderable. How then can I think it sufficient
for those which are infinitely greater, and infinitely
more remote?

[89]   You will now, Sir, perhaps, imagine, that I am

on the point of proposing to you a scheme for a
representation of the colonies in parliament.   Perhaps I might be inclined to entertain some such
thought; but a great flood stops me in my course.
Opposuit natura[1]—I cannot remove the eternal
barriers of the creation.   The thing, in that
mode, I do not know to be possible.   As I med-
dle with no theory, I do not absolutely assert the
impracticability of such a representation.   But I
do not see my way to it; and those who have been
more confident have not been more successful.
However, the arm of public benevolence is not
shortened; and there are often several means to
the same end.   What nature has disjoined in one
way, wisdom may unite in another.   When we
cannot give the benefit as we would wish, let us
not refuse it altogether.   If we cannot give the
principal, let us find a substitute.   But how?
Where? What substitute?

[90]   Fortunately I am not obliged for the ways and
means of this substitute to tax my own unproduc-
tive invention.   I am not even obliged to go to
the rich treasury of the fertile framers of imaginary
commonwealths; not to the Republic of Plato;
not to the Utopia of More; not to the Oceana of
Harrington.   It is before me—it is at my feet,

> —*and the rude swain*
> *Treads daily on it with his clouted shoon.*

---

[1] Nature has opposed.—*Juvenal, Satires, x, 152.*

I only wish you to recognise, for the theory, the ancient constitutional policy of this kingdom with regard to representation, as that policy has been declared in acts of parliament; and, as to the practice, to return to that mode which an uniform experience has marked out to you, as best; and in which you walked with security, advantage, and honour, until the year 1763.

[91] My resolutions therefore mean to establish the equity and justice of a taxation of America, by *grant*, and not by *imposition*. To mark the *legal competency* of the colony assemblies for the support of their government in peace, and for public aids in time of war. To acknowledge that this legal competency has had *a dutiful and beneficial exercise;* and that experience has shown the *benefit of their grants*, and the *futility of parliamentary taxation as a method of supply*.

[92] These solid truths compose six fundamental propositions. There are three more resolutions corollary to these. If you admit the first set, you can hardly reject the others. But if you admit the first, I shall be far from solicitous whether you accept or refuse the last. I think these six massive pillars will be of strength sufficient to support the temple of British concord. I have no more doubt than I entertain of my existence, that, if you admitted these, you would command an immediate peace; and, with but tolerable future management, a lasting obedience in America. I am not

arrogant in this confident assurance. The propositions are all mere matters of fact; and if they are
such facts as draw irresistible conclusions even in
the stating, this is the power of truth, and not any
management of mine.

[93]   Sir, I shall open the whole plan to you, together
with such observations on the motions as may tend
to illustrate them where they may want explanation.
The first is a resolution—"That the colonies and
plantations of Great Britain in North America,
consisting of fourteen separate governments, and
containing two millions and upwards of free inhabitants, have not had the liberty and privilege of
electing and sending any knights and burgesses, or
others, to represent them in the high court of
parliament."—This is a plain matter of fact,
necessary to be laid down, and (excepting the
description) it is laid down in the language of the
constitution; it is taken nearly *verbatim* from acts
of parliament.

[94]   The second is like unto the first—"That the
said colonies and plantations have been liable to,
and bounden by, several subsidies, payments, rates,
and taxes, given and granted by parliament,
though the said colonies and plantations have not
their knights and burgesses in the said high court
of parliament, of their own election, to represent the
condition of their country; by lack whereof they
have been oftentimes touched and grieved by subsidies given, granted, and assented to, in the said

court, in a manner prejudicial to the commonwealth, quietness, rest, and peace of the subjects
inhabiting within the same."

[95]   Is this description too hot, or too cold, too
strong, or too weak? Does it arrogate too much to
the supreme legislature? Does it lean too much
to the claims of the people? If it runs into any of
these errors, the fault is not mine. It is the
language of your own ancient acts of parliament.

> *Non meus hic sermo, sed quæ præcepit Ofellus,*
> *Rusticus, abnormis sapiens.*[1]

It is the genuine produce of the ancient, rustic,
manly, home-bred sense of this country.—I did
not dare to rub off a particle of the venerable rust
that rather adorns and preserves, than destroys,
the metal. It would be a profanation to touch
with a tool the stones which construct the sacred
altar of peace. I would not violate with modern
polish the ingenuous and noble roughness of these
truly constitutional materials. Above all things,
I was resolved not to be guilty of tampering: the
odious vice of restless and unstable minds. I
put my foot in the tracks of our forefathers, where
I can neither wander nor stumble. Determining
to fix articles of peace, I was resolved not to be
wise beyond what was written; I was resolved to
use nothing else than the form of sound words; to

---

[1] This language is not mine, but that taught by Ofellus,
a rustic, but unusually wise.—*Horace, Satires, II, ii, 2, 3.*

let others abound in their own sense; and care
fully to abstain from all expressions of my own.
What the law has said, I say. In all things else I
am silent. I have no organ but for her words.
This, if it be not ingenious, I am sure is safe.

[96]   There are indeed words expressive of grievance
in this second resolution, which those who are
resolved always to be in the right will deny to
contain matter of fact, as applied to the present
case; although parliament thought them true,
with regard to the counties of Chester and
Durham. They will deny that the Americans
were ever "touched and grieved" with the taxes.
If they consider nothing in taxes but their weight
as pecuniary impositions, there might be some
pretence for this denial. But men may be sorely
touched and deeply grieved in their privileges, as
well as in their purses. Men may lose little in
property by the act which takes away all their
freedom. When a man is robbed of a trifle on
the highway, it is not the two-pence lost that con-
stitutes the capital outrage. This is not confined
to privileges. Even ancient indulgences with-
drawn, without offence, on the part of those who
enjoyed such favours, operate as grievances. But
were the Americans then not touched and grieved
by the taxes, in some measure, merely as taxes?
If so, why were they almost all either wholly
repealed or exceedingly reduced? Were they not
touched and grieved even by the regulating duties of

the sixth of George II.?   Else why were the duties
first reduced to one-third in 1764, and afterwards
to a third of that third in the year 1766?   Were
they not touched and grieved by the stamp act?
I shall say they were, until that tax is revived.
Were they not touched and grieved by the duties
of 1767, which were likewise repealed, and which
Lord Hillsborough tells you (for the ministry)
were laid contrary to the true principle of com
merce?   Is not the assurance given by that noble
person to the colonies of a resolution to lay no
more taxes on them, an admission that taxes would
touch and grieve them?   Is not the resolution of
the noble lord in the blue riband, now standing on
your journals, the strongest of all proofs that
parliamentary subsidies really touched and grieved
them?   Else why all these changes, modifications,
repeals, assurances, and resolutions?

97]   The next proposition is—"That from the distance of the said colonies, and from other circumstances, no method hath hitherto been devised for
procuring a representation in parliament for the
said colonies."   This is an assertion of a fact.   I
go no further on the paper; though, in my private
judgment, an useful representation is impossible;
I am sure it is not desired by them; nor ought it
perhaps by us; but I abstain from opinions.

98]   The fourth resolution is—"That each of the said
colonies hath within itself a body, chosen in part, or
in the whole, by the freemen, freeholders, or other

free inhabitants thereof, commonly called the General Assembly, or General Court; with powers legally to raise, levy, and assess, according to the several usage of such colonies, duties and taxes towards defraying all sorts of public services."

This competence in the colony assemblies is certain. It is proved by the whole tenor of their acts of supply in all the assemblies, in which the constant style of granting is, "an aid to his Majesty;" and acts granting to the crown have regularly for near a century passed the public offices without dispute. Those who have been pleased paradoxically to deny this right, holding that none but the British parliament can grant to the crown, are wished to look to what is done, not only in the colonies, but in Ireland, in one uniform unbroken tenor every session. Sir, I am surprised that this doctrine should come from some of the law servants of the crown. I say, that if the crown could be responsible, his Majesty—but certainly the ministers, and even these law officers themselves, through whose hands the acts pass biennially in Ireland, or annually in the colonies, are in an habitual course of committing impeachable offences. What habitual offenders have been all presidents of the council, all secretaries of state, all first lords of trade, all attorneys and all solicitors general! However, they are safe; as no one impeaches them; and there is no ground of charge against them, except in their own unfounded theories.

100]   The fifth resolution is also a resolution of fact—
"That the said general assemblies, general courts,
or other bodies legally qualified as aforesaid, have
at sundry times freely granted several large subsidies and public aids for his Majesty's service,
according to their abilities, when required thereto
by letter from one of his Majesty's principal secretaries of state; and that their right to grant the
same, and their cheerfulness and sufficiency in the
said grants, have been at sundry times acknowledged
by parliament." To say nothing of their great
expenses in the Indian wars; and not to take their
exertion in foreign ones, so high as the supplies in
the year 1695; not to go back to their public con-
tributions in the year 1710; I shall begin to travel
only where the journals give me light; resolving
to deal in nothing but fact, authenticated by
parliamentary record; and to build myself wholly
on that solid basis.

01]   On the 4th of April, 1748, a committee of this
House came to the following resolution:
        "Resolved,
    "That it is the opinion of this committee, *That
it is just and reasonable* that the several provinces
and colonies of Massachusetts Bay, New Hampshire, Connecticut, and Rhode Island, be reim-
bursed the expenses they have been at in taking
and securing to the crown of Great Britain the
island of Cape Breton and its dependencies."

02]   These expenses were immense for such colonies

They were above £200,000 sterling; money first raised and advanced on their public credit.

[103]   On the 28th of January, 1756, a message from the king came to us, to this effect—"His Majesty, being sensible of the zeal and vigour with which his faithful subjects of certain colonies in North America have exerted themselves in defence of his Majesty's just rights and possessions, recommends it to this House to take the same into their consideration, and to enable his Majesty to give them such assistance as may be a *proper reward and encouragement.*"

[104]   On the third of February, 1756, the House came to a suitable resolution, expressed in words nearly the same as those of the message: but with the further addition, that the money then voted was an *encouragement* to the colonies to exert themselves with vigour.   It will not be necessary to go through all the testimonies which your own records have given to the truth of my resolutions, I will only refer you to the places in the journals:

Vol. xxvii.—16th and 19th May, 1757.
Vol. xxviii.—June 1st, 1758— April 26th and 30th, 1759—March 26th and 31st, and April 28th, 1760—Jan. 9th and 20th, 1761.
Vol. xxix.—Jan. 22nd and 26th, 1762—March 14th and 17th, 1763.

[105]   Sir, here is the repeated acknowledgment of parliament, that the colonies not only gave, but

gave to satiety. This nation has formally acknowledged two things; first, that the colonies had gone beyond their abilities, parliament having thought it necessary to reimburse them; secondly, that they had acted legally and laudably in their grants of money, and their maintenance of troops, since the compensation is expressly given as reward and encouragement. Reward is not bestowed for acts that are unlawful; and encouragement is not held out to things that deserve reprehension. My resolution therefore does nothing more than collect into one proposition, what is scattered through your journals. I give you nothing but your own; and you cannot refuse in the gross, what you have so often acknowledged in detail. The admission of this, which will be so honourable to them and to you, will, indeed, be mortal to all the miserable stories, by which the passions of the misguided people have been engaged in an unhappy system The people heard, indeed, from the beginning of these disputes, one thing continually dinned in their ears, that reason and justice demanded, that the Americans, who paid no taxes, should be compelled to contribute. How did that fact, of their paying nothing, stand, when the taxing system began? When Mr. Grenville began to form his system of American revenue, he stated in this House, that the colonies were then in debt two million six hundred thousand pounds sterling money; and was of opinion they would discharge

that debt in four years.   On this state, those
untaxed people were actually subject to the payment of taxes to the amount of six hundred and
fifty thousand a year.   In fact, however, Mr.
Grenville was mistaken.   The funds given for
sinking the debt did not prove quite so ample as
both the colonies and he expected.   The calculation was too sanguine; the reduction was not completed till some years after, and at different times
in different colonies.   However, the taxes after the
war continued too great to bear any addition, with
prudence or propriety; and when the burthens imposed in consequence of former requisitions were
discharged, our tone became too high to resort again
to requisition.   No colony, since that time, ever
has had any requisition whatsoever made to it.

[106]   We see the sense of the crown, and the sense of
parliament, on the productive nature of a *revenue
by grant*.   Now search the same journals for the
produce of the *revenue by imposition*—Where is
it?—let us know the volume and the page—what is
the gross, what is the net produce?—to what
service is it applied?—how have you appropriated
its surplus?—What, can none of the many skilful
index-makers that we are now employing, find any
trace of it?—Well, let them and that rest together.
—But are the journals, which say nothing of the
revenue, as silent on the discontent?—Oh, no! a
child may find it.   It is the melancholy burthen
and blot of every page.

[107]   I think then I am, from those journals, justified in the sixth and last resolution, which is—"That it hath been found by experience, that the manner of granting the said supplies and aids, by the said general assemblies, hath been more agreeable to the said colonies, and more beneficial, and conducive to the public service, than the mode of giving and granting aids in parliament, to be raised and paid in the said colonies." This makes the whole of the fundamental part of the plan.   The conclusion is irresistible.   You cannot say, that you were driven by any necessity to an exercise of the utmost rights of legislature.   You cannot assert, that you took on yourselves the task of imposing colony taxes, from the want of another legal body, that is competent to the purpose of supplying the exigencies of the state without wounding the prejudices of the people.   Neither is it true that the body so qualified, and having that competence, had neglected the duty.

108]   The question now, on all this accumulated matter, is;—whether you will choose to abide by a profitable experience, or a mischievous theory; whether you choose to build on imagination, or fact; whether you prefer enjoyment, or hope; satisfaction in your subjects, or discontent?

109]   If these propositions are accepted, everything which has been made to enforce a contrary system, must, I take it for granted, fall along with it. On that ground, I have drawn the following resolu-

tion, which, when it comes to be moved, will
naturally be divided in a proper manner : ''That it
may be proper to repeal an act, made in the
seventh year of the reign of his present Majesty,
intituled, An act for granting certain duties in the
British colonies and plantations in America; for
allowing a drawback of the duties of customs upon
the exportation from this kingdom, of coffee and
cocoa-nuts of the produce of the said colonies or
plantations; for discontinuing the drawbacks payable on China earthenware exported to America;
and for more effectually preventing the clandestine
running of goods in the said colonies and plantations.—And that it may be proper to repeal an act,
made in the fourteenth year of the reign of his
present Majesty, intituled, An act to discontinue,
in such manner, and for such time, as are therein
mentioned, the landing and discharging, lading or
shipping, of goods, wares, and merchandise, at the
town and within the harbour of Boston, in the
province of Massachusetts Bay, in North America.
—And that it may be proper to repeal an act, made
in the fourteenth year of the reign of his present
Majesty, intituled, An act for the impartial administration of justice, in the cases of persons questioned for any acts done by them, in the execution
of the law, or for the suppression of riots and
tumults, in the province of Massachusetts Bay, in
New England.—And that it may be proper to
repeal an act, made in the fourteenth year of the

reign of his present Majesty, intituled, An act for the better regulating the government of the province of Massachusetts Bay, in New England.— And, also, that it may be proper to explain and amend an act, made in the thirty-fifth year of the reign of King Henry the Eighth, intituled, An act for the trial of treasons committed out of the king's dominions.''

10] I wish, Sir, to repeal the Boston Port Bill, because (independently of the dangerous precedent of suspending the rights of the subject during the king's pleasure) it was passed, as I apprehend, with less regularity, and on more partial principles, than it ought. The corporation of Boston was not heard before it was condemned. Other towns, full as guilty as she was, have not had their ports blocked up. Even the restraining bill of the present session does not go to the length of the Boston Port Act. The same ideas of prudence, which induced you not to extend equal punishment to equal guilt, even when you were punishing, induced me, who mean not to chastise, but to reconcile, to be satisfied with the punishment already partially inflicted.

11] Ideas of prudence and accommodation to circumstances, prevent you from taking away the charters of Connecticut and Rhode Island, as you have taken away that of Massachusetts colony, though the crown has far less power in the two former provinces than it enjoyed in the latter; and though the abuses have been full as great, and as flagrant, in the exempted as in the punished. The same reasons of prudence and accommodation have weight with me in restoring the charter of Massachusetts Bay. Besides, Sir, the act which changes the charter of Massachusetts is in many particulars so exceptionable, that if I did not wish absolutely to repeal, I would by all means desire to alter it; as several of its provisions tend to the subversion of all public and private justice. Such, among others, is the power in the governor to change the sheriff at his pleasure; and to make a new returning officer for every special cause. It is shameful to behold such a regulation standing among English laws.

[112] The act for bringing persons accused of committing murder under the orders of government to England for trial is but temporary. That act has calculated the probable duration of our quarrel with the colonies; and is accommodated to that supposed duration. I would hasten the happy moment of reconciliation; and therefore must, on my principle, get rid of that most justly obnoxious act.

[13] The act of Henry the Eighth, for the trial of treasons, I do not mean to take away, but to confine it to its proper bounds and original intention; to make it expressly for trial of treasons (and the greatest treasons may be committed) in places where the jurisdiction of the crown does not extend.

[114] Having guarded the privileges of local legislature, I would next secure to the colonies a fair and unbiassed judicature; for which purpose, Sir, I propose the following resolution: "That, from the time when the general assembly or general court of any colony or plantation in North America, shall have appointed by act of assembly, duly confirmed, a settled salary to the offices of the chief justice and other judges of the superior court, it may be proper that the said chief justice and other judges of the superior courts of such colony, shall hold his and their office and offices during their good behaviour; and shall not be removed therefrom, but when the said removal shall be adjudged by his Majesty in council, upon a hearing on complaint from the general assembly, or on a complaint from the governor, or council, or the house of representatives severally, of the colony in which the said chief justice and other judges have exercised the said offices."

[115] The next resolution relates to the courts of admiralty. It is this:—"That it may be proper to regulate the courts of admiralty, or vice-admiralty, authorized by the fifteenth chapter of the fourth of George the Third, in such a manner as to make the same more commodious to those who sue, or are sued, in the said courts, and to provide for the more decent maintenance of the judges in the same."

[116] These courts I do not wish to take away; they

are in themselves proper establishments. This court is one of the capital securities of the act of navigation. The extent of its jurisdiction, indeed, has been increased; but this is altogether as proper, and is indeed on many accounts more eligible, where new powers were wanted, than a court absolutely new. But courts incommodiously situated, in effect, deny justice; and a court, partaking in the fruits of its own condemnation, is a robber. The congress complain, and complain justly, of this grievance.

[117] These are the three consequential propositions. I have thought of two or three more; but they come rather too near detail, and to the province of executive government; which I wish parliament always to superintend, never to assume. If the first six are granted, congruity will carry the latter three. If not, the things that remain unrepealed will be, I hope, rather unseemly encumbrances on the building, than very materially detrimental to its strength and stability.

[118] Here, Sir, I should close; but I plainly perceive some objections remain, which I ought, if possible, to remove. The first will be, that, in resorting to the doctrine of our ancestors, as contained in the preamble to the Chester act, I prove too much; that the grievance from a want of representation, stated in that preamble, goes to the whole of legislation as well as to taxation. And that the colonies, grounding themselves upon that

doctrine, will apply it to all parts of legislative authority.

[119]   To this objection, with all possible deference and humility, and wishing as little as any man living to impair the smallest particle of our supreme authority, I answer, that *the words are the words of parliament, and not mine;* and, that all false and inconclusive inferences, drawn from them, are not mine; for I heartily disclaim any such inference. I have chosen the words of an act of parliament, which Mr. Grenville, surely a tolerably zealous and very judicious advocate for the sovereignty of parliament, formerly moved to have read at your table in confirmation of his tenets.   It is true, that Lord Chatham considered these preambles as declaring strongly in favour of his opinions.   He was a no less powerful advocate for the privileges of the Americans.   Ought I not from hence to presume, that these preambles are as favourable as possible to both, when properly understood; favourable both to the rights of parliament, and to the privilege of the dependencies of this crown?   But, Sir, the object of grievance in my resolution I have not taken from the Chester, but from the Durham act, which confines the hardship of want of representation to the case of subsidies; and which therefore falls in exactly with the case of the colonies.   But whether the unrepresented counties were *de jure*, or *de facto*, bound, the preambles do not accurately distinguish; nor indeed was it neces-

sary; for, whether *de jure* or *de facto*, the legislature thought the exercise of the power of taxing,
as of right, or as of fact without right, equally a
grievance, and equally oppressive.

[120] I do not know that the colonies have, in any
general way, or in any cool hour, gone much
beyond the demand of immunity in relation to
taxes. It is not fair to judge of the temper or
dispositions of any man, or any set of men, when
they are composed and at rest, from their conduct,
or their expressions, in a state of disturbance and
irritation. It is besides a very great mistake to
imagine, that mankind follow up practically any
speculative principle, either of government or of
freedom, as far as it will go in argument and logical illation. We Englishmen stop very short of
the principles upon which we support any given part
of our constitution; or even the whole of it together.
I could easily, if I had not already tired you, give
you very striking and convincing instances of it.
This is nothing but what is natural and proper.
All government, indeed every human benefit and
enjoyment, every virtue, and every prudent act, is
founded on compromise and barter. We balance
inconveniences; we give and take; we remit some
rights that we may enjoy others; and we choose
rather to be happy citizens than subtle disputants.
As we must give away some natural liberty, to enjoy
civil advantages; so we must sacrifice some civil
liberties, for the advantages to be derived from the

communion and fellowship of a great empire. But, in all fair dealings, the thing bought must bear some proportion to the purchase paid. None will barter away the immediate jewel of his soul. Though a great house is apt to make slaves haughty, yet it is purchasing a part of the artificial importance of a great empire too dear, to pay for it all essential rights, and all the intrinsic dignity of human nature. None of us who would not risk his life rather than fall under a government purely arbitrary. But although there are some amongst us who think our constitution wants many improvements, to make it a complete system of liberty; perhaps none who are of that opinion would think it right to aim at such improvement, by disturbing his country, and risking everything that is dear to him. In every arduous enterprise, we consider what we are to lose as well as what we are to gain; and the more and better stake of liberty every people possess, the less they will hazard in a vain attempt to make it more. These are *the cords of man*. Man acts from adequate motives relative to his interest; and not on metaphysical speculations. Aristotle, the great master of reasoning, cautions us, and with great weight and propriety, against this species of delusive geometrical accuracy in moral arguments, as the most fallacious of all sophistry.

121] The Americans will have no interest contrary to the grandeur and glory of England, when they are

not oppressed by the weight of it; and they will
rather be inclined to respect the acts of a superintending legislature, when they see them the acts of
that power, which is itself the security, not the
rival, of their secondary importance. In this
assurance, my mind most perfectly acquiesces: and
I confess, I feel not the least alarm from the discontents which are to arise from putting people at
their ease; nor do I apprehend the destruction of
this empire, from giving, by an act of free grace
and indulgence, to two millions of my fellow-
citizens some share of those rights, upon which I
have always been taught to value myself.

[122]   It is said, indeed, that this power of granting,
vested in American assemblies, would dissolve the
unity of the empire; which was preserved entire,
although Wales, and Chester, and Durham were
added to it.   Truly, Mr. Speaker, I do not know
what this unity means; nor has it ever been heard
of, that I know, in the constitutional policy of this
country.   The very idea of subordination of parts,
excludes this notion of simple and undivided unity.
England is the head; but she is not the head and
the members too.   Ireland has ever had from the
beginning a separate, but not an independent,
legislature; which, far from distracting, promoted
the union of the whole.   Everything was sweetly
and harmoniously disposed through both islands
for the conservation of English dominion, and the
communication of English liberties.   I do not see

that the same principles might not be carried into twenty islands, and with the same good effect. This is my model with regard to America, as far as the internal circumstances of the two countries are the same. I know no other unity of this empire, than I can draw from its example during these periods, when it seemed to my poor understanding more united than it is now, or than it is likely to be by the present methods.

[23] But since I speak of these methods, I recollect, Mr. Speaker, almost too late, that I promised, before I finished, to say something of the proposition of the noble lord on the floor, which has been so lately received, and stands on your journals. I must be deeply concerned, whenever it is my misfortune to continue a difference with the majority of this House. But as the reasons for that difference are my apology for thus troubling you, suffer me to state them in a very few words. I shall compress them into as small a body as I possibly can, having already debated that matter at large, when the question was before the committee.

[24] First, then, I cannot admit that proposition of a ransom by auction;—because it is a mere project. It is a thing new; unheard of; supported by no experience; justified by no analogy; without example of our ancestors, or root in the constitution. It is neither regular parliamentary taxation, nor colony grant. *Experimentum in corpore vili*,[1] is a

---

[1] Let us make the experiment on something worthless.

good rule, which will ever make me adverse to any
trial of experiments on what is certainly the most
valuable of all subjects, the peace of this empire.
[125]   Secondly, it is an experiment which must be
fatal in the end to our constitution. For what is
it but a scheme for taxing the colonies in the
antechamber of the noble lord and his successors?
To settle the quotas and proportions in this House,
is clearly impossible. You, Sir, may flatter yourself you shall sit a state auctioneer, with your hammer in your hand, and knock down to each colony
as it bids.   But to settle (on the plan laid down by
the noble lord) the true proportional payment for
four or five and twenty governments, according to
the absolute and the relative wealth of each, and
according to the British proportion of wealth and
burthen, is a wild and chimerical notion. This
new taxation must therefore come in by the back-
door of the constitution. Each quota must be
brought to this House ready formed; you can
neither add nor alter. You must register it. You
can do nothing further. For on what grounds can
you deliberate either before or after the proposition? You cannot hear the counsel for all these
provinces, quarrelling each on its own quantity of
payment, and its proportion to others. If you
should attempt it, the committee of provincial
ways and means, or by whatever other name it will
delight to be called, must swallow up all the time
of parliament.

26]   Thirdly, it does not give satisfaction to the complaint of the colonies. They complain, that they are taxed without their consent; you answer, that you will fix the sum at which they shall be taxed. That is, you give them the very grievance for the remedy. You tell them, indeed, that you will leave the mode to themselves. I really beg pardon: it gives me pain to mention it; but you must be sensible that you will not perform this part of the compact. For, suppose the colonies were to lay the duties, which furnished their contingent, upon the importation of your manufactures; you know you would never suffer such a tax to be laid. You know, too, that you would not suffer many other modes of taxation. So that, when you come to explain yourself, it will be found, that you will neither leave to themselves the quantum nor the mode; nor indeed anything. The whole is delusion from one end to the other.

27]   Fourthly, this method of ransom by auction, unless it be *universally* accepted, will plunge you into great and inextricable difficulties. In what year of our Lord are the proportions of payments to be settled? To say nothing of the impossibility that colony agents should have general powers of taxing the colonies at their discretion; consider, I implore you, that the communication by special messages, and orders between these agents and their constituents on each variation of the case, when the parties come to contend together, and to dis-

pute on their relative proportions, will be a matter
of delay, perplexity, and confusion that never can
have an end.

[128] If all the colonies do not appear at the outcry,
what is the condition of those assemblies, who offer
by themselves or their agents, to tax themselves
up to your ideas of their proportion? The refractory colonies, who refuse all composition, will
remain taxed only to your old impositions, which,
however grievous in principle, are trifling as to
production. The obedient colonies in this scheme
are heavily taxed; the refractory remain unbur-
thened. What will you do? Will you lay new and
heavier taxes by parliament on the disobedient?
Pray consider in what way you can do it. You are
perfectly convinced, that, in the way of taxing,
you can do nothing but at the ports. Now suppose it is Virginia that refuses to appear at your
auction, while Maryland and North Carolina bid
handsomely for their ransom, and are taxed to your
quota, how will you put these colonies on a par?
Will you tax the tobacco of Virginia? If you do,
you give its death-wound to your English revenue
at home, and to one of the very greatest articles of
your own foreign trade. If you tax the import of
that rebellious colony, what do you tax but your
own manufactures, or the goods of some other
obedient and already well-taxed colony? Who has
said one word on this labyrinth of detail, which
bewilders you more and more as you enter into it?

Who has presented, who can present you with a clue, to lead you out of it? I think, Sir, it is impossible, that you should not recollect that the colony bounds are so implicated in one another, (you know it by your other experiments in the bill for prohibiting the New England fishery,) that you can lay no possible restraints on almost any of them which may not be presently eluded, if you do not confound the innocent with the guilty, and burthen those whom, upon every principle, you ought to exonerate. He must be grossly ignorant of America, who thinks that, without falling into this confusion of all rules of equity and policy, you can restrain any single colony, especially Virginia and Maryland, the central and most important of them all.

[129] Let it also be considered, that, either in the present confusion you settle a permanent contingent, which will and must be trifling; and then you have no effectual revenue: or you change the quota at every exigency; and then on every new repartition you will have a new quarrel.

[130] Reflect besides, that when you have fixed a quota for every colony, you have not provided for prompt and punctual payment. Suppose one, two, five, ten years' arrears. You cannot issue a treasury extent against the failing colony. You must make new Boston Port Bills, new restraining laws, new acts for dragging men to England for trial. You must send out new fleets, new armies. All is to

begin again. From this day forward the empire is never to know an hour's tranquillity. An intestine fire will be kept alive in the bowels of the colonies, which one time or other must consume this whole empire. I allow indeed that the empire of Germany raises her revenue and her troops by quotas and contingents; but the revenue of the empire, and the army of the empire, is the worst revenue and the worst army in the world.

[131] Instead of a standing revenue, you will therefore have a perpetual quarrel. Indeed the noble lord, who proposed this project of a ransom by auction, seemed himself to be of that opinion. His project was rather designed for breaking the union of the colonies, than for establishing a revenue. He confessed, he apprehended, that his proposal would not be to *their taste*. I say, this scheme of disunion seems to be at the bottom of the project; for I will not suspect that the noble lord meant nothing but merely to delude the nation by an airy phantom which he never intended to realize. But whatever his views may be; as I propose the peace and union of the colonies as the very foundation of my plan, it cannot accord with one whose foundation is perpetual discord.

[132] Compare the two. This I offer to give you is plain and simple. The other full of perplexed and intricate mazes. This is mild; that harsh. This is found by experience effectual for its purposes; the other is a new project. This is universal; the

other calculated for certain colonies only. This is
immediate in its conciliatory operation; the other
remote, contingent, full of hazard. Mine is what
becomes the dignity of a ruling people; gratuitous,
unconditional, and not held out as matter of bar-
gain and sale. I have done my duty in proposing
it to you. I have indeed tired you by a long discourse; but this is the misfortune of those to
whose influence nothing will be conceded, and who
must win every inch of their ground by argument.
You have heard me with goodness. May you
decide with wisdom! For my part, I feel my mind
greatly disburthened by what I have done to-day.
I have been the less fearful of trying your patience,
because on this subject I mean to spare it altogether
in future. I have this comfort, that in every stage
of the American affairs, I have steadily opposed
the measures that have produced the confusion,
and may bring on the destruction of this empire.
I now go so far as to risk a proposal of my own.
If I cannot give peace to my country, I give it to
my conscience.

[133]   But what (says the financier) is peace to us without money? Your plan gives us no revenue. No!
But it does—For it secures to the subject the
power of REFUSAL; the first of all revenues.
Experience is a cheat, and fact a liar, if this power
in the subject of proportioning his grant, or of not
granting at all, has not been found the richest
mine of revenue ever discovered by the skill or by

the fortune of man. It does not indeed vote you
£152,750: 11: 2¾ths, nor any other paltry limited
sum.—But it gives the strong box itself, the fund,
the bank, from whence only revenues can arise
amongst a people sensible of freedom: *Posita
luditur arca.*[1] Cannot you in England; cannot
you at this time of day; cannot you, a House of
Commons, trust to the principle which has raised
so mighty a revenue, and accumulated a debt of
near 140 millions in this country? Is this principle to be true in England, and false everywhere
else? Is it not true in Ireland? Has it not
hitherto been true in the colonies? Why should
you presume, that, in any country, a body duly
constituted for any function, will neglect to perform its duty, and abdicate its trust? Such a
presumption would go against all governments in
all modes. But, in truth, this dread of penury of
supply, from a free assembly, has no foundation in
nature. For first observe, that, besides the desire
which all men have naturally of supporting the
honour of their own government, that sense of
dignity, and that security to property, which ever
attends freedom, has a tendency to increase the
stock of the free community. Most may be taken
where most is accumulated. And what is the soil
or climate where experience has not uniformly
proved, that the voluntary flow of heaped-up

---

[1] The strong-box (the whole fortune) is put up as a
stake.—*Juvenal, Satires, I, 90.*

plenty, bursting from the weight of its own rich luxuriance, has ever run with a more copious stream of revenue, than could be squeezed from the dry husks of oppressed indigence, by the straining of all the politic machinery in the world.

[134] Next we know, that parties must ever exist in a free country. We know, too, that the emulations of such parties, their contradictions, their reciprocal necessities, their hopes, and their fears, must send them all in their turns to him that holds the balance of the state. The parties are the gamesters; but government keeps the table, and is sure to be the winner in the end. When this game is played, I really think it is more to be feared that the people will be exhausted, than that government will not be supplied. Whereas, whatever is got by acts of absolute power ill obeyed, because odious, or by contracts ill kept, because constrained, will be narrow, feeble, uncertain, and precarious.

> *Ease would retract*
> *Vows made in pain, as violent and void.*

[135] I, for one, protest against compounding our demands: I declare against compounding for a poor limited sum, the immense, evergrowing, eternal debt, which is due to generous government from protected freedom. And so may I speed in the great object I propose to you, as I think it would not only be an act of injustice, but would be the worst economy in the world, to compel the

colonies to a sum certain, either in the way of ran·
som, or in the way of compulsory compact.

[136] But to clear up my ideas on this subject—a
revenue from America transmitted hither—do not
delude yourselves—you never can receive it—No,
not a shilling. We have experience that from
remote countries it is not to be expected. If,
when you attempted to extract revenue from
Bengal, you were obliged to return in loan what
you had taken in imposition; what can you expect
from North America? For certainly, if ever there
was a country qualified to produce wealth, it is
India; or an institution fit for the transmission, it
is the East India Company. America has none of
these aptitudes. If America gives you taxable
objects, on which you lay your duties here, and
gives you, at the same time, a surplus by a foreign
sale of her commodities to pay the duties on these
objects, which you tax at home, she has performed
her part to the British revenue. But with regard
to her own internal establishments; she may, I
doubt not she will, contribute in moderation. I
say in moderation; for she ought not to be per-
mitted to exhaust herself. She ought to be
reserved to a war; the weight of which, with the
enemies that we are most likely to have, must be
considerable in her quarter of the globe. There
she may serve you, and serve you essentially.

[137] For that service, for all service, whether of
revenue, trade, or empire, my trust is in her inter-

est in the British constitution. My hold of the colonies is in the close affection which grows from common names, from kindred blood, from similar privileges, and equal protection. These are ties, which, though light as air, are as strong as links of iron. Let the colonies always keep the idea of their civil rights associated with your government; —they will cling and grapple to you; and no force under heaven will be of power to tear them from their allegiance. But let it be once understood, that your government may be one thing, and their privileges another; that these two things may exist without any mutual relation; the cement is gone; the cohesion is loosened; and everything hastens to decay and dissolution. As long as you have the wisdom to keep the sovereign authority of this country as the sanctuary of liberty, the sacred temple consecrated to our common faith, wherever the chosen race and sons of England worship freedom, they will turn their faces towards you. The more they multiply, the more friends you will have; the more ardently they love liberty, the more perfect will be their obedience. Slavery they can have anywhere. It is a weed that grows in every soil. They may have it from Spain, they may have it from Prussia. But, until you become lost to all feeling of your true interest and your natural dignity, freedom they can have from none but you. This is the commodity of price, of which you have the monopoly. This is the true act of navigation,

which binds to you the commerce of the colonies,
and through them secures to you the wealth of the
world. Deny them this participation of freedom,
and you break that sole bond, which originally
made, and must still preserve, the unity of the
empire. Do not entertain so weak an imagination,
as that your registers and your bonds, your affi-
davits and your sufferances, your cockets and your
clearances, are what form the great securities of
your commerce. Do not dream that your letters
of office, and your instructions, and your suspending clauses, are the things that hold together the
great contexture of the mysterious whole. These
things do not make your government. Dead
instruments, passive tools as they are, it is the spirit
of the English communion that gives all their life
and efficacy to them. It is the spirit of the English constitution, which, infused through the
mighty mass, pervades, feeds, unites, invigorates,
vivifies every part of the empire, even down to the
minutest member.

[138] Is it not the same virtue which does everything
for us here in England? Do you imagine then,
that it is the land tax act which raises your revenue?
that it is the annual vote in the committee of
supply which gives you your army? or that it is the
mutiny bill which inspires it with bravery and
discipline? No! surely no! It is the love of the
people; it is their attachment to their government
from the sense of the deep stake they have in such

a glorious institution, which gives you your army and your navy, and infuses into both that liberal obedience, without which your army would be a base rabble, and your navy nothing but rotten timber.

[39] All this, I know well enough, will sound wild and chimerical to the profane herd of those vulgar and mechanical politicians, who have no place among us; a sort of people who think that nothing exists but what is gross and material; and who therefore, far from being qualified to be directors of the great movement of empire, are not fit to turn a wheel in the machine. But to men truly initiated and rightly taught, these ruling and master principles, which, in the opinion of such men as I have mentioned, have no substantial existence, are in truth everything, and all in all. Magnanimity in politics is not seldom the truest wisdom; and a great empire and little minds go ill together. If we are conscious of our situation and glow with zeal to fill our place as becomes our station and ourselves, we ought to auspicate all our public proceedings on America with the old warning of the church, *Sursum corda!*[1] We ought to elevate our minds to the greatness of that trust to which the order of Providence has called us. By adverting to the dignity of this high calling, our ancestors have turned a savage wilderness into a glorious empire; and have made the most extensive,

---

[1] Lift up your hearts.

and the only honourable conquests, not by destroy-
ing, but by promoting the wealth, the number,
the happiness of the human race. Let us get an
American revenue as we have got an American
empire. English privileges have made it all that
it is; English privileges alone will make it all it
can be.

[140] In full confidence of this unalterable truth, I
now (*quod felix faustumque sit*)[1] lay the first stone
of the temple of peace; and I move you,

"That the colonies and plantations of Great
Britain in North America, consisting of fourteen
separate governments, and containing two millions
and upwards of free inhabitants, have not had the
liberty and privilege of electing and sending
any knights and burgesses, or others, to represent
them in the high court of parliament."

[141] Upon this resolution the previous question was
put, but the resolution failed of adoption;—yeas
78, noes 270.

[142] As the propositions were opened separately in the
body of the speech, the reader perhaps may wish
to see the whole of them together, in the form in
which they were moved for. The first four motions
and the last had the previous question put on them.
The others were negatived. The words in italics
were, by amendment, left out of the motion.

---

[1] May it be happy and fortunate.

"Moved,

43]   "That the colonies and plantations of Great Britain in North America, consisting of fourteen separate governments, and containing two millions and upwards of free inhabitants, have not had the liberty and privilege of electing and sending any knights and burgesses, or others, to represent them in the high court of parliament."

44]   "That the said colonies and plantations have been made liable to, and bounden by, several subsidies, payments, rates, and taxes, given and granted by parliament; though the said colonies and plantations have not their knights and burgesses, in the said high court of parliament, of their own election, to represent the condition of their country; *by lack whereof, they have been oftentimes touched and grieved by subsidies given, granted, and assented to, in the said court, in a manner prejudicial to the commonwealth, quietness, rest, and peace, of the subjects inhabiting within the same.*"

45]. "That from the distance of the said colonies, and from other circumstances, no method hath hitherto been devised for procuring a representation in parliament for the said colonies."

46]   "That each of the said colonies hath within itself a body, chosen, in part or in the whole, by the freemen, freeholders, or other free inhabitants thereof, commonly called the general assembly, or general court; with powers legally to raise, levy, and assess, according to the several usage of such colonies, duties and taxes towards defraying all sorts of public services.''

[147] ''That the said general assemblies, general courts, or other bodies, legally qualified as aforesaid, have at sundry times freely granted several large subsidies and public aids for his Majesty's service, according to their abilities, when required thereto by letter from one of his Majesty's principal secretaries of state; and that their right to grant the same, and their cheerfulness and sufficiency in the said grants, have been at sundry times acknowledged by parliament.''

[148] ''That it hath been found by experience, that the manner of granting the said supplies and aids, by the said general assemblies, hath been more agreeable to the inhabitants of the said colonies, and more beneficial and conducive to the public service, than the mode of giving and granting aids and subsidies in parliament to be raised and paid in the said colonies.''

[149] ''That it may be proper to repeal an act, made in the seventh year of the reign of his present Majesty, intituled, An act for granting certain duties in the British colonies and plantations in America; for allowing a drawback of the duties of customs, upon the exportation from this kingdom, of coffee and cocoa-nuts, of the produce of the said colonies or plantations; for discontinuing the drawbacks payable on China earthenware exported

to America; and for more effectually preventing
the clandestine **running of goods** in the said colonies and plantations.''

0] "That it may be proper to repeal an act, made
in the fourteenth year of the reign of his present
Majesty, intituled, An act to discontinue, in such
manner, and for such time, as are therein mentioned, the landing and discharging, lading or
shipping of goods, wares, and merchandise, at the
town, and within the harbour of Boston, in the
province of Massachusetts Bay, in North America.''

1] "That it may be proper to repeal an act, made
in the fourteenth year of the reign of his present
Majesty, intituled, An act for the impartial administration of justice, in cases of persons questioned
for any acts done by them in the execution of the
law, or for the suppression of riots and tumults in the
province of Massachusetts Bay, in New England.'

2] "That it is proper to repeal an act, made in the
fourteenth year of the reign of his present Majesty,
intituled, An act for the better regulating the government of the province of Massachusetts Bay, in
New England.''

3] "That it is proper to explain and amend an act
made in the thirty-fifth year of the reign of King
Henry VIII., intituled, An act for the trial of
treasons committed out of the king's dominions.''

4] "That, from the time when the general assembly,
or general court, of any colony or plantation, in
North America, shall have appointed, by act of

assembly duly confirmed, a settled salary to the offices of the chief justice and other judges of the superior courts, it may be proper that the said chief justice and other judges of the superior courts of such colony shall hold his and their office and offices during their good behaviour; and shall not be removed therefrom, but when the said removal shall be adjudged by his Majesty in council, upon a hearing on complaint from the general assembly, or on a complaint from the governor, or council, or the house of representatives, severally, of the colony in which the said chief justice and other judges have exercised the said office."

[155]   "That it may be proper to regulate the courts of admiralty, or vice-admiralty, authorized by the fifteenth chapter of the fourth of George III., in such a manner, as to make the same more commodious to those who sue, or are sued, in the said courts; *and to provide for the more decent maintenance of the judges of the same.*"

QUESTIONS ON THE LITERARY AND RHETORI-CAL QUALITIES OF THE SPEECH ON CONCILIATION

One reading of the speech, preferably the first or the second, should be devoted to a study of the literary and rhetorical qualities. The following questions are intended merely to indicate topics for study. The work may be extended as time, and the attainments of the class permit. The order of the questions is perhaps not the best for all classes. Some of the questions may be assigned for reports or brief essays. Numbers in parentheses refer to paragraphs of the speech:

1. What power over words is seen in the use of *event* (1), *delicate* (2), *comprehend* (4), *capital* (12), *occasional* (16), *auspicious* (25), *the genius*, (25), *determine* (36), *sensible* (38), *auspicate* (139)? Compare the etymological meaning of these words with their usual meaning.

2. What argumentative or persuasive force is there in the use of *squabbling* (10), *auction* (10), *indifferently* (13), *partial* (16), *occasional* (16), *adored* (38)? Find other single words which condense a whole argument.

3. One element of Burke's power is his use of specific, concrete, incisive terms. Find examples

in (42) last sentence, (43), (50), (56), or other paragraphs.

4. What characteristic of vocabulary is seen in *such a pass* (5), *play the game out* (5), *produce our hand* (5), *gave so far in to* (6), *a good while* (8), *knock down the hammer* (10), *shot a good deal* (12), *smartness of debate* (42), *mighty well* (42), *have done the business* (45), *are wished to look* (99)? Find other examples.

5. The words which Burke uses close together fit one another's meaning; as, "In this *posture* things *stood*" (5). While his phraseology is not always smooth and nice, he makes effective phrases. Find illustrations in (25), (66), and (72), or in other paragraphs.

6. What does Burke's phraseology owe to the English Bible?

7. Similes, metaphors, and tropes (slightly figurative turns of expression) are very numerous in all of Burke's writings. Cite a few examples from this speech.

8. Burke uses a good many reference words and words of transition and connection to make it easy for the reader to follow his course of reasoning. Mark all there are in (36). Note words and phrases of transition at the beginning of many paragraphs.

9. What evidences of the oratorical temperament are seen in the diction of (1), (4), (15), (25), (30), (43), (45)?

10. Does Burke use the rhetorical question and the exclamation?

11. Find cases of parallelism and balance in sentences. A case of climax. Notice in the Brief Proper the forward march of the three main propositions.

12. Find a wise political maxim expressed in a short sentence in (10), in (13), (45), (59), (65), (66), (83), (88), (96), (120), and (139).

13. Examine the variety in length and structure and kinds of sentences in (25), (45), (55), (56).

14. What characteristics of the introduction are perhaps explained by the fact that he knew his audience to be strongly opposed to his views?

15. Do you find that usually each paragraph deals with only one topic? that it is possible to state the principal thought of each paragraph in a single sentence? What quality of composition is indicated by these facts?

16. In (59) point out the sentence which best expresses the topic. Show how each of the other sentences introduces, or proves, or repeats, or explains, or exemplifies, the main idea.

17. Show in what orderly sequence the ideas of (60) come along. Make a list of them. Notice the proportion of space and the relative prominence given to each of them. Do these correspond with their importance relatively to the thought?

18. In the group (47-64) have we the inductive or the deductive order of thought? How is it in

most of the speech? Is Burke's plan fully
announced at the beginning? Are we kept in sus-
pense as to just what Burke wants? Where do we
find out in full?

19. In (47) Burke says he "would patiently go
round and round the subject, and survey it
minutely in every possible aspect." Burke has
been accused of making too many fine distinctions in
his speeches. Do you think the criticism just? Is
there a distinction made in this speech that is unnec-
essary to the argument? Consult the Brief Proper.

20. Do you find any passages that would sound
too highly oratorical in a speech nowadays? How
about the Latin quotations?

21. Notice a few of the quotations and allusions
and see if there is not a bit of argument or persuasion concealed in each of them. Point it out.
Can you find any purely ornamental passage in
this speech?

22. What passages in this speech indicate especially that Burke was a believer in the "sacredness
of law," and that he reverenced the past? How
often does he appeal to experience as proof of what
he says?

23. If you had read nothing about Burke the
man, could you tell from this speech what some of
his personal qualities (mental, moral, religious)
must have been? Could you tell also whether or
not he had read much? what his favorite books
were? what his political ideals were?

24. Matthew Arnold says that Burke "is so great because, almost alone in England, he brings thought to bear upon politics; he saturates politics with thought." Of what passage in this speech does this statement seem to you to be especially true?

25. "Burke bases his reasoning on facts in human nature." Verify this.

26. Professor Goodrich says that the secret of Burke's richness of thought "consisted, to a great extent, in his habit of viewing things in their *causes*, or tracing them out in their *results*." Verify.

27. Report the steps in the *reductio ao absurdum* in (70-73).

28. What form of argument is used in (81) and (88)? Notice the use of words of comparison, *more*, *less*, *as*, *as much*.

29. Do you find evidences of a powerful imagination in this speech? Do you find any poetic touches?

30. Which of the following adjectives might be used truthfully in speaking of the style of Burke's *Speech on Conciliation*? Cite passages in support of your answer. *Suggestive, picturesque, pathetic, sublime, serious, sincere, keen, judicious, ironical, beautiful, grand, clear, emphatic, precise, simple, colloquial, harsh, intense, diffuse, repetitious.*

A STUDY OF THE LOGICAL STRUCTURE OF THE SPEECH ON CONCILIATION

One reading, preferably the second or the third, may profitably be devoted exclusively to a study of the logical structure of the speech, to an examination of the arguments separately and in their inter-relations. Experience has shown that the arguments will be best appreciated if the paragraphs are condensed into sentences and these sentences are arrayed according to their rank in the argumentative scheme. This kind of work is difficult, but rewards the pupil by giving him a comprehension of the argument such as he can hardly gain in any other way. Fully one-half of the time devoted to this speech may profitably be spent in the making of a Brief. The following suggestions are intended to afford the pupil needed help towards making his Brief. A Brief of Burke's introduction to the speech is given in full in order to illustrate the form preferred. Complete sentences, *reading as reasons*, should everywhere be insisted upon. The numbers given below in parentheses refer to paragraphs of the speech. Directions to the pupil are in brackets. Material not in brackets stands as part of the final Brief. It will pay to adhere to the form and system of numbering suggested, and to draw off a *complete* Brief. Before beginning to make the Brief Proper, let the pupil read the first fourteen paragraphs of the speech, comparing them one by one with the Brief of the introduction given below. Let him note that the main thought of paragraph (1) may be expressed in a single, complete sentence, as (I) below; that the same is true of (2); but that (3) and (4) belong together, forming a contrast; that (5), (6), (7), and (8) also belong together, since they give Burke's excuses for speaking; that (9) gives Burke's proposition; that (10), (11), (12), and (13) belong together because they contrast Burke's plan with Lord North's and show what advantage the former gains from the fact that the latter has been presented; that (13) also adds a new thought (VII below); that (14) closes the introduction by dividing the subject preparatory to the argument proper. Arranging this material in the orderly form of a brief, we have the following.

INTRODUCTION

I. The return of the grand penal bill gives Parliament another opportunity to choose a plan for managing the American colonies (1).

II. Having studied the subject, Burke has arrived at fixed ideas of imperial policy (2).

III. Burke's sentiments have not changed (3); but Parliament has frequently changed its policy, with disastrous results (4).

IV. Burke ventures to address the House, for,
   A. Those opposing the ministry must now produce their plan (5).
   B. Though Burke is reluctant (6), the awful situation makes it his duty to do good if he can (7).
   C. Burke's insignificance will ensure a discussion of his plan wholly on its merits (8).

V. Burke's proposition is to secure peace by removing the grounds of difference (9).

VI. Burke's plan, simple and very different from Lord North's (10), derives advantages from the latter's presentation (11), for,
   A. By accepting Lord North's plan, the House has voted that the idea of conciliation is admissible (11).
   B. By accepting Lord North's plan, the House has voted that the idea of conciliation is admissible *previous* to submission by the colonies (12)
   C. By accepting Lord North's plan, the House has voted that complaints in regard to taxation are not wholly unfounded (12).
   D. Burke's plan is based upon the same principle as Lord North's, that of conciliation (13).

VII. The proposal for peace ought to originate with England, the superior power (13).

VIII. The two leading questions are: Whether England ought to concede; and, What the concession should be; the determination of which depends upon the actual condition and circumstances of America and not upon abstractions or theories (14).

BRIEF PROPER

A. ENGLAND SHOULD CONCILIATE THE AMERICAN COLONIES (15-64), FOR,

  I. The nature and condition of America require conciliation (15), for—[Read (15-30), and having discovered A, B, C and D, set them down in complete sentences reading as reasons for I. Follow the form of the Introduction VI].

  II. Those who advocate force against America are wrong (31), for—[Read (32-35), and having found the reasons, set them down as before].

  III. [Express (36) in form similar to I above. A (37) is followed by reasons, which should be marked 1, 2, etc.]

  IV. This unnatural contention has shaken all fixed principles of government (45-46), for—[Mark the three evil effects A, B and C].

  V. Of the only three ways of dealing with America, we must adopt the third (47), for,

    A. The first way (to remove the causes of the American spirit) is impossible (48-57) for —[Find the reasons, marking them 1, 2, etc., and if reasons for 1, or 2, etc., are given, mark them a, b, c, etc.].

    B. [Supply the thought. Keep the form of sentence used for A just above.]

    C. The third way, to comply with the American spirit, we must, therefore, adopt (64).

B. THE MEASURES OF CONCILIATION ADOPTED SHOULD SATISFY THE AMERICAN COMPLAINT AGAINST TAXATION (65-88), FOR,

  I. To please any people, you must give them the boon they ask (65).

  II. To refuse satisfaction on the ground of a legal

right to tax is illogical (66), for—[Read (66-68) to find reasons.   Reason A is implied in the questions in (66)].

III. [Express (70) in the form of sentence used in II, just above, "To refuse," etc.   Read (71-74) for reasons.]

IV. [Express (75) in the form of sentence used in II. Reason A (last sentence of 75).   Reason B (76).]

V. Such satisfaction would be in accordance with four great constitutional precedents (77-78), for —[Phrase A, B, C, D, (79-87), and E (88), with reasons, if any are given, under each].

C. SATISFACTION OF THE AMERICAN COMPLAINT IS POSSIBLE WITHOUT GRANTING REPRESENTATION IN PARLIAMENT (89 AND 90), FOR,

I. Parliament would give satisfaction (in part) by ceasing to *impose* taxes and declaring the competency of colonial *grants* (91), and record-ing its belief in the following resolutions (92-93).

A. That the colonies are not represented in Parliament (93).

B. That the colonies have been grieved by taxes (94-95), for,

1, It is a grievance to be hurt in one's privi-leges, irrespective of the money involved (96).   [Supply 2, 3, etc., from the rest of paragraph (96).]

[C (97), D (98), D 1 (99), E (100), E 1 (100-105), F (106-108).]

II. Parliament would give satisfaction (in part) also by repealing the Acts named in the Resolution (109), for,

A. The Boston Port Bill is unjust (110) for— [Find in (110) two reasons, 1 and 2].

[B (111), C (112), D (113), with reasons, if any are given.]

III. [Read (114-118). Express the thought in the form of sentence used in I and II, just above.]

IV. The argument that the grievance of taxation extends to all legislation cannot stand (118), for—[Read to (121), finding reasons].

V. [Express (122) in the form of sentence used in IV, just above.]

VI. The foregoing plan of satisfying the American complaint is better than Lord North's (123). for—[Read (124-132), drawing off the reasons].

VII. [Express (133) in the form of IV, just above. Find reasons.]

CONCLUSION

I. The real ties that bind the colonies to the Empire are not laws, but ties of loyalty and affection (137-138).

II. [Find in paragraph (139) a single sentence that expresses the thought.]

III. Burke therefore moves the following resolution [as given in (140-155)].

NOTES

¶ [1] *Sir.* The Speaker of the House of Commons.
austerity of the Chair. The severe impartiality of the speaker.
my motion. At the end of the speech.
grand penal bill. Lord North's bill (proposed Feb. 10, 1775) entitled "An Act to restrain the Commerce of the Provinces of Massachusetts Bay and New Hampshire, and Colonies of Connecticut and Rhode Island, and Providence Plantation, in North America, to Great Britain, Ireland, and the British Islands in the West Indies; and to prohibit such Provinces and Colonies from carrying on any Fishery on the Banks of Newfoundland, and other places therein mentioned, under certain conditions and limitations." By this bill thousands of New England fishermen were to be reduced to beggary.
is to be returned to us. The Lords wanted the bill amended so that it should apply to other American colonies besides those of New England.
mixture of coercion and restraint. A contemptuous name for the Grand Penal Bill. *incongruous* with conciliation. Burke cannot mean that coercion is incongruous with restraint.

¶ [2] *blown about.* Ephesians iv, 14. In this and adjacent lines Burke refers to the rapid changes of opinion in and out of Parliament as to the best way to deal with the colonies. Parliament passed the Stamp Act one year and repealed it the next.

¶ [3] *At that period.* The repeal of the Stamp Act. The vote stood 275 for the repeal, 161 against.

¶ [4] *Everything administered as remedy.* The Tea-Tax, Boston Port Bill, Massachusetts Colony Bill, Transportation Bill, and Quebec Act.
her present situation. The colonies were preparing for war. Lexington was fought within a month.

138

¶ [5] *a worthy member.* Mr. Rose Fuller. A year before, Burke had delivered his speech on American Taxation on a motion by Mr. Fuller to repeal the tax on tea.

American committee. The whole House of Commons sitting as a committee on American affairs. A "committee of the whole" chooses its own chairman—some member, not the speaker.

our former methods. The methods of "the opposition," (the minority party or parties) which had been confined to criticism of measures proposed by the ministry (chosen from the majority party).

platform. Plan.

¶ [6] *seat of authority.* Here means the government ministry.

disreputably. Ill-timed propositions discredit the maker of them.

¶ [7] *paper government.* Merely on paper, theoretical, incapable of being put into operation because not practical. A reference perhaps to the scheme of government which the philosopher Locke drew up for Carolina.

separated from the execution. A plan which is not to be executed by the one who drafted it.

my caution. My disinclination to bring forward a plan.

laid hold on. 1 Timothy vi, 19. Hebrews vi, 18.

¶ [8] *natural.* Arising from ability. *adventitious.* Arising from rank, title, wealth, or other external circumstance.

¶ [9] *discord fomented from principle.* Burke refers to the principle underlying Lord North's project (see note on ¶ 10) to weaken the colonies by dividing them into two classes.

juridical. Purely legal and technical, without reference to equity and justice. Compare ¶ 66.

shadowy boundaries. Limits of power in regard to the right to tax. The Tories held that the right to tax the colonies was implied in Parliament's general right of legislation. The radical Whigs held to the contrary. The Whigs of Burke's type waived the question of legal right and declared that it was inexpedient to tax the colonies whether Parliament had the legal right, or not.

unsuspecting confidence. Italicized because used by the Congress at Philadelphia in 1774 to express the state of feeling in the colonies after the repeal of the Stamp Act.

¶ [10] *the project.* February 20, 1775, Lord North brought in resolutions, entitled " Propositions for Conciliating the Differences with America," which were agreed to by the House February 27, as follows: "That when the governor, council, or assembly, or general court, of any of his Majesty's provinces or colonies in America, shall propose to make provision, according to the condition, circumstances, and situation of such province or colony, for contributing their proportion to the common defense (such proportion to be raised under the authority of the general court or general assembly of such province or colony, and disposable by Parliament), and shall engage to make provision also for the support of the civil government and the administration of justice, in such province or colony, it will be proper, if such proposal shall be approved by his Majesty and the two Houses of Parliament, and for so long as such provision shall be made accordingly, to forbear, in respect of such province or colony, to levy any duty, tax, or assessment, or to impose any further duty, tax, or assessment, except such duties as it may be expedient to continue to levy or impose, for regulation of commerce: the net produce of the duties last mentioned to be carried to the account of such province or colony respectively "

noble lord Lord North, a Knight of the Garter, wore the badge of that order, a blue ribbon.

colony agents. The colonies not having direct representation in Parliament engaged agents to watch legislation and otherwise look after colony interests there. Franklin was once such an agent for Pennsylvania, Massachusetts, Maryland, and Georgia, and Burke himself was agent for New York for a short time.

¶ [11] *registry.* In the House journals.

resolution. Lord North's project. The advantage lay in the use of the word " conciliating " in the title of Lord North's resolutions.

menacing front of our address. Feb. 9, 1775, Parliament had presented an address to the king declaring that no part of his authority over the colonies should be relinquished. For the use of *front*, see Othello I, iii, 80.

bills of pains and penalties. Two of these bills were the Boston Port Bill and the Grand Penal Bill.

ideas of free grace. Voluntary concessions.

¶ [12] *it has declared . . . and has admitted.* By the very fact of agreeing to Lord North's resolutions.

¶ [13] *I shall endeavour to show.* See ¶ 124 to ¶ 131.

¶ [14] *the object.* The colonies.

¶ [16] *minima.* Trifles. *De minimis non curat lex,* the law takes no account of trifles. The logical subject of this sentence is America.

¶ [17] *ground has been trod.* The matter has been discussed. *some days ago.* March 16.

person. Mr. Glover, esteemed a poet in his day.

at your bar. The bar is a rod across the entry to the chamber in which Parliament sits. Members and officers alone are admitted within the bar.

¶ [19] *comparative state.* A statement making comparisons.

on your table. Officially before you.

Davenant. Appointed inspector-general of exports and imports in 1705.

¶ [20] *The African.* The slave trade, principally; hence rightfully regarded by Burke as a branch of England's export trade to the colonies, since the slaves were taken to the colonies and sold.

¶ [25] *It is good, etc.* Mark ix, 5.

Clouds, indeed, etc. Addison, *Cato* V. i: —

   The wide th' unbounded Prospect lies before me
   And Shadows, Clouds, and Darkness, rest upon it.

Lord Bathurst. Born 1684; took his seat in Parliament in 1705; died Sept., 1775.

angel. The guardian angel.

the fourth generation, the third prince. George the Third was the grandson of George the Second.

made Great Britain. By the Act of Union (1707) England and Scotland became one.

higher rank. Bathurst was made Earl in 1772.

a new one. His son was made Lord Chancellor with the title of Baron Apsley the year previous.

taste of death. Matthew xvi, 28.

¶ [28] *deceive the burthen.* Lighten the burden by beguiling the burden-bearer. A Latinism (*fallere*).

¶ [29] *corn.* Grain.

Roman charity, etc. A reference to an old Roman story, one version of which is that Cymon, having been condemned to die by starvation, was kept alive by his daughter Xanthippe, who visited him in prison and nourished him from her own breasts.

¶ [30] *Serpent.* A constellation within the Antarctic Circle.

Falkland Island . . . . national ambition. Spain and England disputed the ownership of these islands in 1770. Many Englishmen thought them not worth fighting for. Spain yielded before war broke out. These islands were supply stations for whalers.

run the longitude. Literally, sail east or west; here, southwest.

vexed. Agitated. A Latinism (*vexare*).

¶ [31] *complexions.* Temperament.

military art. Several army men in the House, including General Burgoyne, had made speeches advocating the use of force against the colonies.

wield the thunder. An allusion to Jupiter and his thunderbolts. Lord North as prime minister might be said to "wield the thunder of the state."

¶ [34] *British strength.* The colonists were Englishmen. It was for their rights as Englishmen that they were contending.

a foreign enemy. France or Spain might take advantage of England when England was engaged in war with her colonies.

¶ [35] *Our ancient indulgence.* Our former kindness to the colonies.

our penitence. Our recent policy of coercion.

¶ [37] *restive.* Properly means stubborn. Here used in the sense of *restless.*

¶ [38] *when.* In the times preceding the establishment of the Commonwealth.

sensible object. An object capable of being perceived by the senses.

ancient commonwealths. Rome and the states of Greece.

several orders. Several ranks or classes of the people.

greatest spirits. Pym, Hampden, Vane.

¶ [39] *popular.* Controlled by the people.

¶ [40] *of that kind.* Dissenters from the Church of England.

dissidence of dissent. Dissent carried to the extreme. Matthew Arnold uses this phrase (of Hooker's) in *Culture and Anarchy*, ch. I, 21.

the establishments. The state churches.

¶ [41] *Gothic.* Teutonic.

were the Poles. Burke uses the past tense *were* because he is speaking of the Poles before 1772, the year of the Partition of Poland between Austria, Russia and Prussia.

¶ [42] *by successful chicane.* Gen. Gage forbade the colonists from calling any town meetings after August 1, 1774. They evaded the order by adjourning over the first to a time definite; by continuing this process of keeping alive the same adjourned meeting they obviated the necessity of *calling* a meeting. Consult Hosmer, *Samuel Adams.* 322-323.

friend. Thurlow, the attorney-general, who was taking notes of Burke's speech. *on the floor.* The lowest tier of benches, occupied by members of the cabinet.

¶ [43] *winged ministers of vengeance.* Ships, which are compared to the eagle that carried Jupiter's thunderbolts in its pounces, or talons.

So far shalt thou go. Job xxxviii, 11.

¶ [45] *with all its imperfections, etc.* Hamlet I, v

Lord Dunmore. Governor of Virginia

¶ [46] *abrogated the ancient government of Massachusetts.* In 1774, an act of Parliament forbade the people of Massachusetts to hold town meetings except by permission of the royal governor; gave to the royal governor the power to appoint and remove at pleasure all judges and magistrates, including sheriffs, and charged the sheriffs with the duty of summoning jurymen. The object was of course to make the courts mere creatures of the royal will.

¶ [47] *inconvenient.* Troublesome.

giving up the colonies. This was seriously proposed and defended by Dr. Tucker, Dean of Gloucester, in 1774, on the ground that England would have the trade of the colonies whether she owned them or not, if she offered them the best markets.

¶ [50] *English Tartars.* The allusion is to the hordes of Tartars and Mongols who under Genghis Khan (1160–1227) and Timour (1336–1405) swept over Asia, conquering as they went.

Increase and multiply. Paradise Lost X, 730. Genesis i, 28.

children of men. Psalms cxv, 16.

wax and parchment. Legal forms.

¶ [53] *your speech.* Matthew xxvi, 73. Judges xii, 6.

¶ [54] *burn their books.* Acts xix, 19.

chargeable. Expensive.

¶ [55] *has had its advocates.* Dr. Johnson in his pamphlet, *Taxation no Tyranny,* favored this plan. In 1775, Governor Dunmore of Virginia threatened to try this plan.

other people. For instance, the Romans after Cannae armed 8,000 slaves and allowed them to earn their freedom by valor.

¶ [56] *their refusal.* In the years preceding the Revolution attempts were repeatedly made by the legislatures of Virginia and other southern colonies to restrict the slave trade, but the English government prevented the restriction each time, in the interest of English traders.

Angola. On the west coast of Africa. Noted for its activity in the slave trade.

Guinea captain. The captain of an English ship engaged in the Guinea trade.

¶ [57] *Ye gods, etc.* Quoted as an example of hyperbole in chapter xi of *The Art of Sinking in Poetry* written by Arbuthnot, Pope and Swift.

¶ [59] *Sir Edward Coke.* At Raleigh's trial for treason (1603), Coke, then attorney general, assailed Raleigh in most unjust and brutal terms: " Thou art a monster!" " Thou hast a Spanish heart, and thyself art a spider of hell!" Raleigh was accused of having a part in the plots against James the First.

¶ [60] *ex vi termini*. From the meaning of the word; from the force of the term.

¶ [61] *civil litigant*. A party to a suit in which a right (not a crime) is the subject of dispute; in this case, England's right to tax the colonies. *a culprit*. Because, if Parliament decides that it has the right to tax, America is *criminal* in resisting.

¶ [62] *those very persons*. The majority in Parliament. *declaring a rebellion*. February 9, 1775. *formerly addressed*. February 13, 1769. *addressed*. Petitioned the king.

¶ [66] *startle*. Are startled. Startle is now used transitively.

great Serbonian bog, etc. Paradise Lost II, 592–594. The great Serbonian bog is Lake Serbonis between Damiata, a town near the mouth of the Nile and Mt. Casius, on the coast farther east.

¶ [67] *unity of spirit*. Ephesians iv, 3.

¶ [69] *a revenue act*. The Stamp Act, repealed in 1766. *understood principle*. As an act for raising revenue, not for controlling trade.

¶ [70] *American financiers*. Members of Parliament who still think America can be made to yield England a revenue.

have further views. Will keep asking for further concessions.

trade laws. The Navigation Acts were the chief trade laws. *a gentleman, etc.* Mr. Rice.

¶ [71] *acts of navigation*. One of these acts secured to England the lion's share of the carrying trade by forbidding every other nation to bring to England or to her colonies any thing but the actual products of that nation; another forbade the colonies to send exports, directly, anywhere except to England or to other English colonies; by another, all exports from the colonies to England must be shipped in American or English vessels.

¶ [73] *the pamphlet.* Written by Dean Tucker. See note to ¶ 47.

¶ [75] *But the colonies will go further.* The objection of Burke's opponents.

¶ [78] *Philip the Second.* King of Spain. 1556–1598

English constitution. Partly defined in the preceding paragraph; not a single document like the Constitution of the United States, but all of the important state documents (such as Magna Charta and the Bill of Rights) as well as the historical traditions, precedents, long established principles, institutions, and the enacted laws.

¶ [79] *English conquest.* See Green, *Short History of the English People*, ch. vii, sec. viii.

Magna Charta. See Green, *Short History of the English People*, ch. iii, secs. ii and iii.

all Ireland. English settlers in Ireland kept within certain limits called the Pale. " Beyond the Pale " English laws and liberties were not enjoyed.

Sir John Davis (or Davies). Published in 1612 the book to which Burke refers, entitled *Discovery of the true Causes why Ireland was never entirely subdued nor brought under Obedience of the Crown of England until the Beginning of his Majesty's happy Reign.* (James the First was king.)

vain projects. See Green, *Short History of the English people*, ch. vii, sec viii.

changed the people. By settling parts of Ireland with English and Scotch.

altered the religion. From Catholic to Protestant.

deposed kings. Charles the First and James the Second.

altered the succession. By the Act of Settlement (1701) the House of Hanover came to the throne in 1714.

usurpation. The protectorate of Cromwell 1649–1660.

restoration. Charles the Second, 1660.

Revolution. In 1688 Parliament deposed James the Second and put William, Prince of Orange, on the throne.

lucrative amount. Irony.

¶ [80] *Henry the Third.* 1216–1272. *Edward the First.* 1272–1307.

lords marchers. Lords of the marches (border-lands) between England and Wales. Each had the authority of a king in his own district, which he had conquered.

¶ [81] *question on the legality.* Burke implies that an act of Parliament was required, instead of a mere instruction (an executive order).

¶ [82] *rid.* Rode.

¶ [83] *day-star.* 2 Peter i, 19.

¶ [84] *county palatine.* A county in which the owner had royal power.

¶ [85] *Shown,* predicate of *inhabitants.*

where. Whereas.

disherisons. Deprivations.

commonwealth. Common weal, common welfare.

ne. Nor.

¶ [86] *Reject it, etc.* These questions show the kind of treatment that had been accorded to the addresses and petitions of the American colonists.

temperament. Modification.

¶ [88] *Judge Barrington.* Appointed justice of three counties in Wales in 1757.

But your legislative authority is perfect, etc. (So my opponents say.)

legislative authority. Authority, or legal right, to legislate.

But America is virtually represented. (So my opponents say.) *virtually represented.* When the radical Whigs argued that representation is a "natural right" and that there could legally be "no taxation without representation," the Tories replied that America was "virtually" represented. The doctrine of virtual representation implied that even though the Americans had no members of Parliament of their own choosing, yet Parliament as constituted represented the Americans since every member of Parliament is in duty bound to care for the interests, not merely of his own constituency, but of the whole empire.

¶ [89] *arm - - - shortened.* Isaiah lix, 1.

¶ [90] *rude swain.* Milton, *Comus,* 634 635. Milton has "*dull* swain." *clouted shoon.* Shoes with big-headed nails in the soles.

1763. The first year of the Grenville administration, which passed the Stamp Act.

¶ [91] *by grant.* By the voluntary contribution of the colonies through act of their own legislative assemblies.

by imposition. By a tax imposed by Parliament.

¶ [92] *temple of British concord.* An allusion to the temple which the Romans dedicated to Concord.

¶ [93] *fourteen.* Including the Province of Quebec.

description. The particular names.

¶ [94] *like unto.* Matthew xxii, 39.

¶ [95] *touch with a tool.* Exodus xx, 25.

wise beyond what was written. 1 Corinthians iv, 6.

form of sound words. 2 Timothy i, 13.

¶ [96] *the sixth* (act) *of George II.* An act for the better securing of the trade of his Majesty's sugar colonies in America.

Lord Hillsborough. Secretary of State for the Colonies, 1768 to 1772.

¶ [99] *an aid.* Originally an aid was a grant of money voluntarily made by a tenant to his lord.

those who have been pleased, etc. Grenville, Prime Minister 1763–5, and originator of the Stamp Act.

if the crown could be responsible. Whatever the sovereign of England does officially is done by the advice of his ministers, who are held responsible. In this sense "The King can do no wrong."

the council. The Privy Council. A body of selected advisers to the sovereign.

first lords of trade. A committee of the Council.

¶ [100] *so high.* So far back.

¶ [105] *misguided people.* The English.

unhappy system. That of taxing America instead of depending on America's voluntary grants.

state. Statement.

those untaxed people. Those who were *said to be* untaxed.

requisitions. Demands for money addressed by the English Secretary of State to the colonies, to be met by voluntary grants. This process involved an act of the colonial legislatures, which might refuse a grant. Burke repeatedly insists on the fundamental distinction between money thus secured and taxes imposed by Parliament without any act of the colonial legislatures.

¶ [107] *utmost rights.* Taxing the unrepresented.

another legal body. The colonial legislature.

¶ [109] *clandestine running.* Smuggling.

¶ [110] *during the king's pleasure.* The Boston Port Bill provided that the King was to decide when the port should be reopened.

restraining bill. Another name for the Grand Penal Bill See note to ¶ 1.

partially. Unfairly.

¶ [111] *far less power.* The crown did not have the veto power in Connecticut and Rhode Island.

returning officer. The officer who summoned the jury. The object of the regulation was to secure verdicts favorable to the crown.

¶ [112] *temporary.* The act was to continue in force three years from June 1, 1774.

¶ [115]. *courts of admiralty.* These had jurisdiction in the case of offenses committed on the sea, including cases of smuggling, which were tried without a jury.

more decent maintenance. These judges were paid out of the fines which they imposed; hence the temptation to excessive fines and numerous seizures.

¶ [120] *logical illation.* In the *Speech on American Taxation* Burke uses the expression, "too much logic and too little sense."

immediate jewel. Othello, III, iii, 156.

a great house . . . slaves haughty. Juvenal, *Satires*, V, 66, has: *Maxima quaeque domus servis est plena superbis.* Every great house is full of haughty slaves.

cords of man. Hosea xi, 4.

Aristotle . . . cautions us. Aristotle, *Ethics*, I, iii.

¶ [121] *superintending legislature.* In his *Speech on American Taxation* Burke says: "The Parliament of Great Britain sits at the head of her extensive empire in two capacities: One as the local legislature of this island, providing for all things at home, immediately, and by no other instrumen than the executive power.—The other, and I think her nobler capacity, is what I call her *imperial character;* in which, as from the throne of Heaven, she superintends all the several inferior legislatures, and guides and controls them all, without annihilating any."

¶ [122] *a separate . . . legislature.* The Irish Parliament was abolished in 1800. See Green, *Short History of the English People*, ch. x, sec, iv.

¶ [123] *promised.* See ¶ 13.

the proposition of the noble lord. See note to ¶ 10.

¶ [125] *ante-chamber of the noble lord.* The Cabinet or a committee of the Cabinet.

state auctioneer. Compare ¶ 10.

back-door. Some committee.

quarrelling. Compare ¶ 10.

¶ [126] *quantum.* Amount.

¶ [128] *composition.* Agreement. A creditor "compounds" with an insolvent debtor for a less sum than the debt.

you give its death-wound. Because England already taxed imported tobacco, and Virginia tobacco could not endure another tax.

¶ [130] *treasury extent.* A writ for valuing lands of a debtor that are to be taken in payment of his debt.

empire of Germany. Not the present empire; the Holy Roman Empire is meant.

¶ [132] *certain colonies only.* Only those that should choose to contribute instead of being taxed.

¶ [133] *debt.* An evidence of the government's credit.

¶ [134] *Ease would retract, etc.* Paradise Lost, iv, 96–97. Milton has *recant*, not *retract*.

¶ [136] *return in loan.* The reference is to Lord North's Indian Act of 1773, by which £1,400,000 were loaned to the East India Company at four per cent, and the annual payment of £400,000 by the company to the government was remitted until the loan should be discharged.

enemies. France and Spain.

¶ [137] *ties . . . light as air.* Compare Othello III, iii, 322–324.

links of iron. Compare Julius Caesar I. iii, 94–95.

grapple. Compare Hamlet I, iii, 63.

turn their faces. Compare 1 Kings viii, 44, 45. Daniel vi, 10.

of price. Compare Matthew xiii, 46.

cockets . . . clearances. Most of the nouns of this sentence are custom-house terms. A cocket is a custom-house seal or certificate. A clearance is a permit for a vessel to sail.

spirit. Compare Æneid vi, 726, 727. Dryden's translation, 982–985:

> One common soul
> Inspires and feeds and animates the whole.
> This active mind, infus'd through all the space,
> Unites and mingles with the mighty mass.

¶ [138] *land tax act*. An act passed by Parliament each year for raising revenue.

mutiny bill. A bill providing for the discipline of army and navy, passed by Parliament each year.

¶ [139] *profane herd*. Horace, *Odes*, III, i, 1: *Odi profanum vulgus*. I hate the profane herd.

all in all. 1 Corinthians xv, 28.

¶ [141] In the first edition of this speech, which has been followed by almost all editors, this paragraph reads as follows: "Upon this resolution, the previous question was put, and carried;—for the previous question 270, against it 78." The Parliamentary History, however, gives the ayes as 78 and the nays as 270 and adds: "So it passed *in the negative*." All of the resolutions advocated by Burke in this speech failed of adoption. This result was brought about by an adverse vote on the "previous question." In America, "I move that the previous question be now put," stops debate at once, and a vote is immediately taken on the question "Shall the previous question be now put?" If the vote is adverse, debate may continue. But in England, if the vote is adverse to putting the previous question, debate *cannot* continue, and the previous question (which is the *main* question) is considered to be disposed of in the negative. By moving the "previous question" and then defeating the motion, Burke's opponents escaped the need of committing themselves on the main issues raised by his resolutions.

moving the "previous question" and then defeating the motion, Burke's opponents escaped the need of committing themselves on the main issues raised by his resolutions.

INDEX

Numbers in brackets refer to paragraphs; other numbers refer to pages

153